ALTERNATIVES

Alternatives

PROPOSALS FOR AMERICA FROM THE DEMOCRATIC LEFT

EDITED BY IRVING HOWE

ESSAYS BY

IRVING HOWE

BOB KUTTNER

BARBARA EHRENREICH *and*

FRANCES FOX PIVEN

GORDON ADAMS

ROBERT LEKACHMAN

MICHAEL HARRINGTON

PANTHEON BOOKS *New York*

Library of Congress Cataloging in Publication Data
Main entry under title:

Alternatives, proposals for America from the
democratic left.

Contents: Reaganism / Irving Howe—Jobs / Bob
Kuttner—Creating real national security / Gordon
Adams—[etc.]
1. United States—Economic policy—1981– —
Addresses, essays, lectures. 2. United States—Politics
and government—1981– —Addresses, essays, lectures.
I. Howe, Irving.
HC106.8.A425   1984   338.973   83-19503
ISBN 0-394-53369-0
ISBN 0-394-72268-X (pbk.)   Rev.

Book design by Margaret M. Wagner

CONTENTS

ALTERNATIVES

I. REAGANISM: THIS TOO WILL PASS

IRVING HOWE

EVER since Ronald Reagan's election as President in 1980, we have been experiencing in America what might be called a partial counter-revolution. Reagan's election brought to the United States a political phenomenon it has never really known in the twentieth century: an ideological government.

The conservatism of Richard Nixon was more sophisticated, but also more opportunistic, than that of Reagan. In behalf of commonplace bourgeois ends, Nixon was ready to accept a quantity of social legislation and a degree of government intervention into the economy. Nixon liked to suppose himself an American Disraeli; Reagan's scope of references is largely confined to Hollywood and the rhetoric he picked up as a propagandist for General Electric, one of our more vehemently anti-union corporations.

Simplistic in thought but skillful in expression, Reagan seems really to believe his own catchwords: "Get the government off our backs," and so forth. In reality, the interpenetration of government and business, state and economy has continued these past several decades as an all but inevitable process. What has changed is, first, that with regard to this process we have been subjected to a barrage of deception by conservative ideologues who still talk as if laissez faire were a serious option, and second, that the social purpose of government intervention has shifted from helping (not enough) the poor to enriching still further the rich.

Reagan came into office with a clear programmatic intent. The maximum program of his administration was to repeal the New Deal, to demolish the semblance of a welfare state that we have. Insofar as that was clearly not feasible, the Reaganites worked hard to put through their minimum program: to reduce the welfare state to an even feebler shadow of its former self. Give the devils their due. To a notable extent, the Reaganites did realize these minimum goals. They celebrated the virtues of "rugged individualism," the "free market," and a minimalist state that would not interfere with corporate profits but continue to deliver enormous tax bonanzas and defense contracts to its corporate allies.

Once or twice the Reagan administration overreached itself. When it toyed with the idea of cuts in Social Security benefits, it discovered that many Americans who had voted for Reagan, perhaps in response to his slogan about getting the government off our backs, also wanted to be sure they kept their pension and unemployment benefits. Even those Americans who shared the yearning for a return to a simpler, precorporate America also resisted the destruction of crucial elements of the welfare state. Especially popular were those programs that benefited large segments of the population, like unemployment insurance and Social Security; far more vulnerable were those which helped mostly the poor, like free school lunches and aid to dependent mothers. It was at the latter programs that Reagan hacked away, often with a kind of mean-spiritedness belying the image he has created of being a nice guy. He isn't.

Would a second term make Reagan bolder in trying to go beyond the minimum program of the right, or would he and his cronies decide to let well enough alone, concluding that for them a stripped-down welfare state is tolerable? No one can be sure. We may hope never to find out. But meanwhile I think it important to stress one point: the sheer deceit, which may also be self-deceit, in the talk about getting government out of economic life. All that talk did not lead to a significant decline of government intervention; it only changed its character. The policies of the Federal Reserve Board, for instance, constitute a decisive intervention into economic life. The readiness of the federal government to bail out the Lockheed, Penn Central, and Chrysler corporations is quite as decisive an intervention as a program to provide jobs for the unemployed would be—if such a program for the jobless were adopted. The central decision of the 1980s will be whether to direct the government's economic role toward regressive or progressive ends, toward an entrenchment of corporate power or a renewal of liberal goals.

How severe is the damage already done to the welfare state? To answer the question even briefly, we need first to draw a preliminary model—more outline than picture—of what we mean by a welfare state.

The welfare state represents a phase in the development of modern capitalist society—a capitalist society in part transformed and somewhat humanized, as a result of the pressures of democratic insurgency, first and foremost by the labor movement. And it is a capitalist society made somewhat more rational in its operation, for its sophisticated defenders now recognize that the survival of the business class requires that the government clip some of its powers.

The welfare state coexists with and sustains the domination of the capitalist economy by regulating politically the power of property owners to run their businesses. There are minimum wages, environmental regulations, safety provisions in the workplace, rules concerning monopoly, taxes for Social Security, and so on. Creating a certain tension between government and economy, the welfare state acts to save capitalism from its own self-destructive excesses.

Indisputably, the welfare state has eased the lives of millions of people. If these achievements are today taken for granted, that is because an earlier generation fought hard for them. Nor are these trivial matters, despite what extremists of right and left may say. Such social gains rest on a new, if not yet adequate, sense of communal responsibility, an awareness that the creed of "possessive individualism" no longer provides us, if ever it did, with adequate norms for a humane existence. And a crucial part of this new sense of communal responsibility has been the political and social acceptance of new insurgent constituencies: the unions first of all, but also the blacks, the women's movement, the gays, and others.

This improvised and rickety welfare state is always being undermined, renovated, pulled apart, and patched together. It is a result of social improvisation and compromise. It is, most of all, an arena for regulated social conflict. Abstractly the model of the welfare state may signify an inner equilibrium; in reality, it is a much sloppier affair, with constant tensions, breakdowns, and conflicts. No sooner, for instance, does the corporate sector regain its confidence, in good measure as a result of first aid provided by the welfare state, than it sets to work vindictively trying to choke the life out of its benefactor.

A welfare state can't remain stationary for very long. In a welfare state, you have to do a great deal of running just to stand still. Frequent interjections of social reforms are needed to cope with the decay of earlier reforms (the fact, for example, that the rich learn to get around tax provisions or corporations learn to bend safety regulations). The Reagan administration did severe damage to our fragile state not only by cutting existing social programs but by failing to undertake new ones required by the socio-economic crisis of the early 1980s. It failed to set up serious programs for public jobs for the unemployed. It ignored completely the tragic situations created in our industrial heartland as a result of plant shutdowns. It allowed major American cities to rot away. All of these Reaganite decisions constituted a "principled" refusal to act upon new, extremely serious problems. In the years to come we will surely pay for this in social turmoil and human suffering.

Why, come to think of it, did Reagan win?

· Reagan won, in part, because his opponent stood for little or nothing. Before Jimmy Carter there had been a number of Democratic administrations continuing—some more, some less—the spirit of social reform that marked Franklin Roosevelt's presidency, especially during the mid-thirties. By the time Carter became President, this heritage of social liberalism had thinned out —not so much intellectually, though that also, but politically, as a force within the Democratic party. Carter's nomination symbolized, at least partially, a defeat of liberalism in the Democratic party; his stay in office completed that process. When Reagan ran against Carter, it must have seemed to many voters that they had to choose between a principled conservative and a meandering technocrat without strong convictions.

· Reagan won, in part, because the Carter people, like most politicians who boast of their pragmatism, turned out not to be very good pragmatists. During the crisis over the Iran hostages, Carter's staff failed to appreciate sufficiently that there remained among Americans a strong sentiment of nationalism, battered during the Vietnam War and therefore all the less patient with the thought of another battering in Iran. Exactly what the Carter administration could or should have done about this is really a question; the Reagan attack on its Iran policies was demagogic. Nevertheless, that attack worked.

· Reagan won, in part, because he was the beneficiary of a social process that had been gathering momentum for some years: the very successes—genuine successes!—of the welfare state slowly give rise to new and difficult problems. Now, it may be that some difficulties of the Carter administration were accidental. The tremendous rise in oil prices exacted by OPEC could not be blamed on Carter, though it had a strong immediate effect in the form of rising inflation. Some of the socio-economic problems in the welfare state, however, were probably *systemic* in character—especially those which appeared as stagflation, that stubborn mixture of little or no economic growth, increasing structural unemployment, and persistent inflation. We don't yet have a theory of the welfare state sufficiently complex to be able to specify its distinctive inner contradictions in the way that various existing theories specify the distinctive inner contradictions of classical capitalism. A certain point seems to be reached in the growth of the welfare state where its uneasy coexistence with private capital breaks down and serious tensions between the two develop.

The Reaganites cleverly harped on the troubles of the welfare state and the charms of "the good old days." They had the advantage of being able to put forward a few easily grasped and potent slogans, while Carter had to fall back upon the argument (truthful, no doubt, but seldom a help in politics) that modern political economy is complex and not to be grasped with slogans lettered on 3″ x 5″ cards.

Upon taking office, Reagan tried to act on his ideas, which led to the fiasco of supply-side economics—and that, in turn, to the worst recession since the Second World War. As I write in late 1983, a recovery seems on the way, but if it acquires any strength, it will probably lead to a new round of inflation. And recovery or not, we appear certain to suffer from a deplorable level of unemployment.

· Reagan won, in part, because of his use of ideology. The received wisdom of the pollsters and political scientists, who point out that the swing of votes in 1980 was only marginal, calls into question the claim that there occurred a major shift to the right.

· But of course the shift in votes was only marginal (in the American political system it can seldom be more than that). Nevertheless, the fervor that Reaganism aroused among the rich, the middle classes, and even some intellectuals testifies that he somehow touched feelings deeply lodged in the American psyche. He touched a still very strong yearning for a return to "an earlier America"—one that was grounded in the depths of American myth. To be sure, if there had been no stagflation and unemployment to indicate troubles within the welfare state, this appeal to "an earlier America" might never have gained so strong a response.

The earlier America invoked by the right was associated with the ethos of native individualism: a world that had few regulations and fewer laws, that gave a fellow plenty of space, that enabled him to determine his own fate without having to worry about hers, and that rewarded hard work, persistence, and intelligence. Forming the strongest component of our collective consciousness, this myth has inspired both the best and worst in American experience; and no mere rational demonstration that it never matched reality is seriously going to weaken its impact.

During the past half-century, the experience of millions of Americans showed that this myth was a poor guide for coping with life in an advanced industrial society. What could it say to those selling apples on city streets during the early 1930s, or those appalled by the Vietnam War in the late 1960s? When social change became inevitable—it was called the New Deal—the individualist myth *in its extreme and crude form* took a beating, though in fact there is no reason to think that a more modulated and humane individualism, one recognizing the interplay between self and society, could not be reconciled with social welfare measures. Still, there were large portions of the American upper strata which, even as they submitted to the New Deal and profited from its ministrations, secretly held it in contempt—indeed, hated it. Only when the benefits of the welfare state proved substantial enough to restore their confidence did the American business classes feel able to reassert "possessive individualism," which is to say, Reaganism. And one sign of this reassertion is the way that, in recent years, that savagery which in the past had been reserved for foreigners is now turned by arrogant young conservatives against "soft-hearted liberals, lazy blacks, whining women, perverse gays." Gradgrind and Bounderby, Podsnap and Veneering, Bumble and Merdle—Dickens's phantasms are now made flesh. What is the attitude of the Reagan administration to the millions of jobless but that of Podsnap who would not "fly in the face" of a "comfortable . . . Providence" in order to ward off want?

The Reaganite moment has a peculiar sordidness. It's as if the rapacity of the old robber barons had been resurrected, as if the most callous notions of Social Darwinism were back with us. Visions of community that were to relieve the heartlessness of a moneyed society become an object of mockery. The reigning god —cruel and unappeasable—is the Market.

A finer and gentler strand of American individualism, one which recognizes that no individual can survive except in the linked circles of community, is for the moment subordinate in our culture. It is the strand of individualism most beautifully personified in Melville's Ishmael, who upon encountering the dark-skinned sailor Queequeg embraces him as a brother. This strand of American sensibility can never be suppressed for very long; it will come back.

The loose association of trade unions, liberal groups, blacks, and Jews comprising the New Deal coalition seemed broadly based and a genuine reflection of what many Americans wanted. It had significant achievements to its credit. It had managed to legitimate among many Americans the reality, if not always the idea, of the welfare state. I offer a few speculations about why it came apart. There is bound to be much unevenness of gratification in such coalitions. This leads to a conflict of purpose. There has been a striking disparity in the gains made by segments of the skilled working class and the Jewish community, on the one hand, and the blacks, on the other—indeed, it was in the late 1960s that some analysts began speaking about the black experience as a "frustrated revolution." Many American blacks felt cheated and turned to slogans about "black power"—in its extreme form, a chimera that released their anger without slaking their desires. The blacks, however, continued to provide liberal candidates with a higher percentage of votes than that provided by any other group in the country—though the total number of voters among the blacks was still far from what it could be. Among the Jews there appeared a conservative impulse, partly because of issues concerning Israel but also because they were starting to respond to their improved socio-economic status. And among labor unionists there began, likewise, to appear somewhat conservative inclinations, especially regarding "social issues" like crime, abortion, "permissiveness," and so forth.

There was also a new tension created by the rise of previously muted constituencies whose demands sometimes came into conflict with those of more traditional elements in the labor-liberal coalition. Women, environmentalists, lesbians, gays, Chicanos—a host of new groups put forward legitimate demands; but sometimes they did this in styles that ruffled the feelings or seemed even to threaten the economic interests of blue-collar workers and middle-class liberals. The very successes of the welfare state contributed to a partial disintegration of the popular alignment that had brought it into being. In the long run, that may be good. The dynamic of progress in the welfare state—never smooth—requires that new constituencies articulate their claims for entitlement. In the short run, there was division.

There were other reasons for the severe disruption. The most glaring was, of course, the Vietnam War. Many young people and intellectuals who would normally have been solidly within the liberal-left coalition found themselves opponents, not only politically but morally, of a war they regarded as unjust. That some unions supported the war only worsened this split.

The divisions within the labor-liberal community that the war evoked have not yet been healed. You could almost set down a "rule" here: except in times of severe recession, moral responses to perceived outrages in foreign policy and in the treatment of minority groups are likely to be so strong within "communities of conscience" that these responses will often override shared economic interests. If the Reaganite intervention in Central America continues, we may again suffer this kind of division.

Let me mention still another reason for the coming-apart of the labor-liberal coalition (it's not entirely broken—only damaged). During the early 1960s, the country experienced a moment of good feeling. Sentiments of racial fraternity were in the air. By the late 1960s, blacks felt outraged. Searing conflicts broke out between black groups (a few committed to an extremism of imagery) and some of their allies of yesterday. The idea of "going it alone" took hold among black youth and intellectuals. Meanwhile, an ugly sentiment spread through white America. And all through the 1970s, many Americans became obsessed with the problem of crime—often with reason. The popular imagination was struck by the reality of the black "underclass," a seemingly permanent mass of black youth without jobs, prey to pathology, and living off their wits. The popular imagination was struck by this problem, often in distorted and nasty ways; but the society at large did almost nothing to cope with it.

In such an atmosphere it was inevitable that there would follow a breakdown of relations between black and white, even among those sharing political views. Only in the early 1980s did all this start to change.

We're living, right now, through a strange moment. The political right has had the initiative for several years. Outwardly, the country shows few signs of social idealism or rebellious impulse. Occasionally, as on the issue of nuclear arms, large numbers of people bestir themselves, but only now and then, and not in a sustained way. Perhaps the country has not yet recovered from the traumas of the Vietnam War years.

Political life has been steadily changing—in many ways, for the worse—over the past several decades. Consider only the effects of TV: nowadays candidates for office seldom even pretend to make a sustained speech developing their ideas, if any, and responding to the platform of their opponents. Everything is pitched to a two-minute blurb. When TV arranges a "debate" between candidates, it's often a farce, the very format making for an excruciating superficiality. Almost gone is the kind of public meeting that used to be a feature of our political life during the years of my youth—I mean the kind of meeting where a candidate was expected to say something. As political and social issues become more complex, the articulation of opinion becomes more simplistic.

The sources of this apathy are not completely understood, but I suspect it has something to do with the steady encroachment of those social arrangements and values that a few decades ago were lumped under the heading of "the mass society"—that is, the tendency toward homogenization and atomization of the population, the breakdown of coherent political publics, and so forth. A country in which millions of people are glued to the TV set for some twenty hours a week is not a good bet for those who would like to see sustained political participation.

Our parties have never had much coherence of program or thought, but with the significant exception of the Reagan people, there is less and less effort in current politics to organize around common interests and opinions. It has grown fashionable to preen oneself on being an "independent," and all too often this means to have no clear commitment to any views or to have only a "high-minded" concern with certain moral issues while looking down one's nose at the needs of "the unwashed." The general trend, then, has been toward breakup, withdrawal, confusion. In such a moment, the vacuum that is thereby created in political life tends to be filled by whichever force can present itself as decisive and strong—for the moment, the Reagan right.

Apart from Reagan's true believers, however, there has been a process of "dealignment," the disintegration of coherent publics, groups, constituencies. The political analyst Everett Ladd has shrewdly described the process of "dealignment":

> A realignment encompasses the movement of large numbers of voters across party lines, establishing a stable new majority coalition. In a dealignment, by contrast, old coalitional ties are disrupted, but this happens without some new stable configuration taking shape. Voters move away from parties altogether. . . .

These difficulties are aggravated by one of the most disturbing aspects of American political life—the failure of millions of citizens even to vote. In presidential years, writes political analyst Walter Dean Burnham, the pool of nonvoters comes to nearly half the eligible citizens. As I write, a major effort is under way to get some of these people to register and vote. Let this effort succeed and the results would be tremendously valuable for the liberal left.

It is a moment of uncanny quiet. There are still, as I write, millions of unemployed. So far, the unemployed have not yet been heard from—does having another wage-earner in many of their families make things a little easier? does unemployment insurance cushion their loss? does TV lull their minds? We don't know, but if earlier history is any guide, the stillness of this moment could change quickly. America is a volatile country.

The immediate questions, then, for the American liberal left are, first, whether a new coalition can be put together to defend the welfare state (which also, necessarily, means to extend it), and second, what would constitute an adequate socio-economic program for such a coalition (which also, necessarily, has to go somewhat beyond traditional liberal proposals).

How are things on our side? The unions are in trouble—some of them, unfortunately among the best, in deep trouble. The inherent limitations of collective bargaining are evident: how can you bargain when your job disappears, when your factory shuts down, when your whole industry starts to wobble? Ordinary, pure-and-simple unionism seems less and less capable of confronting such difficulties, and it will take some time before unions make an adjustment.

The formal economic program of the AFL-CIO is very good, a part of it anticipating ideas advanced in the essays that follow; but that program is little known, even among union members, and no sufficient effort has been made to put it on the agenda of national discussion. On the other hand, the unions are going more and more deeply into Democratic party politics, and that's probably a good thing, especially if not confined to top-level maneuvering. But even in trouble, even with diminished strength, the unions still constitute the single most substantial and important element of any new political alignment on the liberal side. The unions aren't, by themselves, enough; but without them, little if anything can be done.

A very hopeful sign is the recent upsurge of black political activity, coming as it does after a number of years in which the black community seemed to be living a somewhat ingrown and introspective existence. There are new black leaders in the cities, shrewd and tough; yet their capacities are very limited because the crucial decisions affecting millions of people are not made at the municipal, not even at the state, levels. Still, the election of black mayors in such major cities as Chicago is a sign of renewed confidence, keener political tactics, a readiness to bargain in the here and now. All of this means that the traditional allies of the blacks won't be able to take them for granted, as in the past they sometimes did. But the crucial question regarding the participation of blacks in a new alliance is a simple one: can enough blacks who haven't bothered to vote in the past be persuaded that voting matters?

There are now a good many groups, either in or near the liberal-labor alliance, that are passionately fixed upon a single issue—sometimes to the point where they refuse to compromise with potential allies. This is, indeed, the result of strength gained from earlier victories—the welfare state has enabled minority groups to assert themselves as they could not do before. But it is also a sign of more recent defeats.

Let me cite a crucial instance. One of the few deeply encouraging developments of the last several years has been the rise of insurgent sentiment within the Catholic community, most dramatically visible in the statement of the bishops on nuclear policy. But many liberal or left Catholics continue to hold the traditional position of their church on abortion, and this of course brings them into collision with the women's movement. The issue is a serious one, it stirs deep feelings on both sides, and it could be a major barrier to putting together a new coalition. Is there any way to get around this barrier? Neither side is likely to convince the other, and it would be foolish for either to try strong-arming the other. So far as I can see, there is only one way of handling this problem: we must accept the reality of abiding differences on certain "social issues" and acknowledge—especially at a moment when the duration and depth of the economic recovery seems uncertain while unemployment will very likely remain high—that the focus of a progressive coalition must be on the kind of economic issues discussed in the following essays in this book. Around these overriding concerns it is quite possible for many Catholics to join with others. Let's, then, try to reach agreement about such matters while accepting, more or less gracefully, that we can't agree on abortion, school prayer, and the like.

The fundamental problem, however, remains programmatic. You can't win with "nothing" against "something," even if that "something" is threadbare, foolish, and reactionary. Reaganism may strike many of us as an ideological caricature; we may expose it as a rationale for the new greed of the New Right. But the fact remains: Reaganism certainly is "something"; it offers a more or less coherent view of the world. Those "centrist" Democrats who think they can slip into victory by not offending anyone, which means by expressing as few opinions as possible, are deluding themselves. I don't mean that the country is ready for all the programs outlined in this book; no, it isn't. But if the opposition to Reaganism is to gather strength, then it must, at the least, avoid looking like Carter politics all over again.

We are living through a *partial* exhaustion of the liberal tradition in American politics. Not, I think, a rejection of its basic values, but rather a loss of clarity and confidence regarding specific policies. There is plenty of reason for this: the times are hard, the times are confusing, and honest people of all persuasions are often unsure of what to say.

I think that what is happening can be put this way: we are entering the second stage of the welfare state (Michael Harrington, in his essay, speaks of a third stage, but he means pretty much the same thing). In the early 1930s, the labor-liberal left knew just what it wanted to propose: the first measures creating a welfare state. For about half a century, this gave impetus to the progressive coalitions. Now we need new and more complex— which is to say, more controversial—proposals. Such proposals, like the one for "social control of credit," cut deeply into traditional corporate "prerogatives" and move us a little bit closer to popular control over economic life. And as we enter this second stage of the welfare state, we don't have the advantage, on our side, of simple and readily grasped slogans—at least not yet. There will be a lot of preparatory work to do before we get to that stage, and this book is one contribution toward that end.

Each of the authors in this book looks with care and cogency at a number of our most urgent immediate problems—not all the problems, of course, but those which are central for moving forward to what I'd call a new and better New Deal. Bob Kuttner confronts the crucial question of jobs, the likelihood that even if the economic recovery of 1983 continues there will still be millions of people "structurally" unemployed. He offers a number of specific, immediate proposals—the kind that can be acted upon now even as they would move us closer to a better future. Barbara Ehrenreich and Frances Fox Piven focus on the needs of American women, the newest and potentially very powerful constituency, with special reference to the large number of women hovering about the poverty line or poorly paid. They, too, make specific suggestions—in this case, for eradicating the condition that has come to be called "the feminization of poverty." Gordon Adams deals with our vastly inflated defense budget, and while recognizing the need for a realistic defense policy, offers proposals for cutting this budget so that funds can be released for social purposes. Robert Lekachman then takes up the problems of financing the measures that the other contributors to this book are proposing. Finally, Michael Harrington analyzes the need—one that will be with us for the next few decades—for a coordinated program of social planning, democratic in character and egalitarian in stress. My own task, in this book, has been to lay out the context, the social and political background, within which these writers advance their proposals.

We make no pretense to being exhaustive. Foreign policy, for example, is beyond the scope of this small book. There are omissions, also, with regard to domestic affairs: the situation of black Americans, the problems of environment, the decay of the cities, and so forth. Still, many of the proposals offered suggest parallel policies in other areas. The stress on programs for creating full employment, for instance—genuinely full employment, not the fake version of it now being touted by the Reaganites—is crucial for American blacks. Full employment and expanded governmental services, such as advocated in the essays by Kuttner and by Ehrenreich and Piven, may not be sufficient for coping with the socio-economic problems of the black community; but they form, at the very least, a necessary basis for doing that.

Some contributors to this book think of themselves as left-liberals and others as democratic socialists. No matter. What we are proposing here is not a program for long-range social reconstruction —that's for another book, and in any case, not on the immediate agenda. What we are proposing here is a left-liberal or, as they might say in Europe, a social democratic approach for the next decade.

The proposals we advance here range in character from immediate, short-range suggestions—such as some of Bob Kuttner's ideas on creating new jobs—to what might be called deep-going "structural reforms" within a capitalist society. Even these proposals are likely to meet with strong resistance, not only from conservative opponents (which is only natural) but also from politicians who believe the road to success is paved with evasion.

We don't, therefore, suppose that our suggestions are likely to be adopted as a whole, or immediately, by the Democratic party or even its liberal wing. But we believe they offer workable starting-points for those who want a progressive renewal in American life.

Programs can be worked on, debated, improved. Still, something else is needed—a new surge of social energy. Perhaps someone has written persuasively to explain why at certain moments—the mid-1930s, say, and the early 1960s—there appeared in the United States an entire new mood of hope, aspiration, commitment, idealism. At such moments, people long immobilized or even apathetic come suddenly to feel that they can move—*move beyond the limits of the "given."* Suddenly they think not only of themselves as individuals, but as members of a community. Suddenly the old phrases about liberty, equality, fraternity take on a new life.

Why this happens when it does and why there are intervening periods of apathy, conservatism, even cynicism, I cannot say with any assurance. One thing seems likely: there is constant change, and when the next phase of aspiration and energy comes, we are likely to wonder how it was that we didn't see it sooner. Meanwhile, we have to work to make it come.

II. JOBS

BOB KUTTNER

AMERICA'S current job problem is, unfortunately, not the result of a cyclical downturn that will be remedied by the upswing of the business cycle. Unless radically new policies are developed, unemployment is likely to remain at 8 to 10 percent for the next decade. Since the late 1960s, each recovery of the economy from recession has produced a higher unemployment rate than the previous one. There is substantial evidence of long-term structural changes in the American economy, which suggest that we can sustain a "recovery" of sorts with unemployment rates scarcely touched. At this writing, the Dow Jones is roaring along at close to 1,300 while unemployment persists at 10 percent.

Besides the obvious problem of not enough jobs, there is an equally distressing, if more subtle, problem of not enough *good* jobs. As the economy shifts from a production base to services, information, and high technology, more jobs are being created at the extremes of the labor force and fewer in the middle. A factory economy, particularly when factories are unionized, produces millions of relatively high-wage production jobs. A service economy needs engineers and executives at one extreme—and millions of secretaries, fast-food workers, sales clerks, waiters, computer operators, and janitors at the other. If public policy is floundering on the issue of high unemployment, it has barely even noticed the more difficult issue of job distribution and content. If the middle of the labor market is eroding, it becomes increasingly difficult to maintain the United States as a middle-class society.

Before turning to remedies, it is important to look at the structural changes in the economy, for the job shortage and the "good job" shortage are closely related, and both have multiple causes. These causes include demographic shifts, the pressures of foreign trade, technology, the decline of the public sector, and the effects of a worldwide labor surplus on domestic jobs and wages.

First, consider the demographics. During the 1970s, an unprecedented number of women and young people entered the labor force. The young people happened to be alumni of the baby boom generation. Some women were motivated partly by feminism; then as real wages and living standards fell after 1973, many more were compelled to find work by the need to maintain household purchasing power. As recently as 1960, only 30 percent of married women with children worked. By 1980, the percentage was 57 percent. Even among mothers with children under 6 years old, today nearly half hold jobs. Fully two-thirds of the growth in the labor force during the 1970s was accounted for by women workers.

Although the economy grew at a somewhat slower rate during the 1970s than during the 1960s, it generated an astonishing 21 million additional jobs—50 percent more new jobs than during the 1960s. Even this formidable accomplishment, however, was insufficient for the burgeoning labor force, which grew by over 24 million. Simple arithmetic dictated that 3 million more people had no jobs at all. Further, the mismatch between the swollen labor force and the number of jobs created a classic supply-and-demand problem: managers could now attract workers for lower wages. More workers were accommodated than ever before, but the price for this was a drop in real wages.

After 1973, this effect was compounded by the slowdown in real economic growth. At the same time that real wages dropped for both men and women, more and more women poured into the labor force, putting even more downward pressure on wages. This huge bulge in the labor force, of course, is a one-time phenomenon; the baby boom will not be repeated for a very long time; nor can female labor-force participation rates jump to nearly male rates more than once. But it will be thirty years before these effects subside.

The high unemployment/low wage syndrome has been compounded by the effects of international trade. As recently as 1960, trade accounted for only about 5 percent of the Gross National Product. The United States, and Western Europe to a surprising degree, were able to build domestic economies based on high wages, because each was substantially insulated from pressures from low-wage areas of the globe. European exports were not yet a threat to America's high-wage labor market, because American technology still dominated most basic industries. Superior American technology was not a significant danger for Europe's labor market, because the dollar was extremely overvalued in relation to European currencies. Partly because of the strong dollar and partly as a deliberate policy in the spirit of the Marshall Plan, American manufacturers did not export substantial amounts of industrial products to Europe; rather, they exported capital. They built plants in Europe, which provided jobs for European workers and transferred technology to European industry.

As a consequence, there was a historical moment when nations on both sides of the Atlantic could enjoy high real growth, rising real wages, and a costly welfare state. The postwar social contract defied the Marxian picture of reserve armies of unemployed workers and falling real wages, mainly because each political economy existed in splendid isolation.

The world since the late 1960s is radically different. Until the last two decades, underdeveloped countries served mainly as sources of raw materials for the products of advanced industrial countries and as markets for a portion of those products. Comparative advantage, in practice, worked very much to the advantage of the industrial nations, because terms of trade were very favorable and because the industrial nations got to export the high-value-added products. Since the late 1960s, however, Third World countries have increasingly acquired branch plants of western multinational firms and have begun developing their own export industries. Technology and capital have become mobile. Almost anything that can be produced in the United States can be produced in a high-technology island of the Third World at wages that are absurdly low by American standards. The world's most modern steel mill is currently in Nigeria; it pays its workers about $200 a month. Korean shipbuilding workers are half as productive as Swedish workers, but they work at one-eighth of the wages.

This new reality puts a whole new cast on the Ricardian concept of comparative advantage. As originally propounded, the theory of comparative advantage was based on what economists call "factor endowments"—a country's natural advantages in arable land, raw materials, climate, or plentiful labor force. If Honduras has a climate suitable for growing bananas, and Canada has plentiful reserves of aluminum ore and cheap hydroelectric power, it would be patently absurd for Canada to attempt to grow bananas or for Honduras to dig for bauxite. But comparative advantage today is increasingly based on whose workforce will work for the lowest wages, or who is cleverest at appropriating the newest technology and penetrating other countries' markets.

"Protection," which is increasingly difficult to define (industrial policy is a form of protectionism, isn't it?), is often condemned as irrational. But by passively submitting to a comparative advantage based on ever cheaper labor—all in the name of some idealized notion of free trade—we beggar ourselves.

The new exporting Third World countries, by combining high technology with low labor costs, contribute in several respects to unemployment and falling real wages in the United States. First, they replace American jobs. Second, they put pressure on employed American workers to moderate their wage demands. Third World competition has given American industry a whole new rationale for resisting unionism and decent pay scales. There is now a cottage industry of business school experts advising us that America's chief problem is that we've priced ourselves out of world markets. Surely, however, we can't expect American workers to lower their wage levels all the way to the standards of a dollar an hour and less that prevail in much of the Third World.

As the Great Depression made clear, falling real wages create a classic Keynesian problem as well. They depress worker purchasing power and consequently depress aggregate demand. Thus, the purported gains of free trade may be illusory. If shirts manufactured in Taiwan are cheaper than shirts produced in North Carolina, American consumers gain. But if the American textile worker displaced by the foreign-made shirt remains unemployed, or is employed at a lower-value-added occupation, then the economy as a whole may lose. Conventional economics does not factor into the same equation the efficiency gain of trade and the output loss of idle physical and human capital. Whether the gain outweighs the loss is settled empirically, not axiomatically as the free trade purists would have it. It depends entirely on whether the idled factors of production are re-employed, and at what activities. If yesterday's steelworker is today's cashier at McDonald's, then the entire economy is producing less value added per worker, and workers as a group have less disposable income.

In addition to the pressures of demographic shifts and foreign competition, unemployment persists because of revolutionary changes in technology. For the first time since the industrial revolution, we seem to be entering a period when technology could truly wipe out more jobs than it creates. More subtly, technology seems to be eliminating high-paid production jobs and eroding the middle of the labor force, with severe consequences for America's future as a middle-class society.

The most difficult problem of all is the interaction of trade and technology, as it affects the labor market. America's problem, we are told, is a lack of competitiveness: our workers are overpaid and our technology is obsolete. For many business conservatives and "Atari Democrats" alike, the remedy is productivity. By making our production processes more efficient, we will restore American industry to a position of competitiveness, which in turn will restore economic growth and produce the jobs that the economy needs.

But the literal definition of higher productivity is more output for less labor input. By this definition, increasing productivity means fewer jobs, unless the economy is growing very rapidly. Thus, the productivity paradox: the more American industry becomes increasingly productive in order to compete in world markets, the more Americans are thrown out of work. Economic planners in every country are urging policy makers to emulate Japan: to reduce unemployment by targeting capital investment on export winners. As long as only Japan was pursuing this strategy, it had no trouble exporting its unemployment; Japan currently has a trade surplus in industrial products of over $100 billion! But every country cannot solve its unemployment problem by exporting it. There is room for only one or two Japans.

Finally, we have a version of the 1930-style Keynesian problem of unemployment breeding more unemployment and putting downward pressure on wages, especially at the low end. When eleven or twelve million people are out of work, they are a drag on aggregate demand as well as consumers of transfer payment dollars. They consume, but do not produce. The federal deficit we have today is not sufficient to stimulate the economy out of recession, because it is a deficit born of tight money, lost tax revenues, and stagnant national output, not a deficit associated with a program of economic stimulation. With 8 to 10 percent of the labor force out of work, real wages decline, especially at the low end of the workforce which can more easily be replaced with the unemployed. Unions have a more difficult time bargaining for wage increases at a time of high unemployment. There is new credibility to the idea that "excessive" wages are themselves responsible for high unemployment, although the Great Depression and Keynes's work on aggregate demand should have laid that idea to rest. The minimum wage, a force for egalitarian pay structures, was once 54 percent of the average wage. It has now dropped to about 38 percent.

The erosion of the middle of the labor market, while closely related to the problem of high structural unemployment, is a distinct cause for concern. Studies by U.S. Department of Labor economists suggest that wage inequality has been widening since at least the late 1950s. The most comprehensive of these studies, by Bureau of Labor Statistics economists Peter Henle and Paul Ryscavage (published in the *Monthly Labor Review*, May 1980), contrasted the distribution of wages in 1958 with that in 1977. Henle and Ryscavage found that at the twentieth percentile of earnings (the bottom fifth), male workers increased their earnings by 130.6 percent in current dollars. But at the eightieth percentile (the top fifth), earnings increased by 206.7 percent. Highly skilled and trained workers, professionals, and executives simply had more bargaining power and more prospect of full-time work than their lower-skilled workmates at the bottom of the pay scale.

The polarization of wages is also compounded by shifts in the distribution of occupations. Several independent empirical studies by an ideologically diverse assortment of economists have calculated that the rapidly growing service occupations have created pay structures steadily growing more unequal, while only the declining manufacturing sector offers a distribution of wages that is both relatively egalitarian and stable. *Services: The New Economy* (1981), a book-length study by Thomas M. Stanback, Jr., et al (published by Allanheld Osmun), concluded that the service economy in general exhibits polarized wages, while the declining production and construction sectors offered relatively higher wages and a wage structure that was far less skewed to the extremes. Construction and production work accounted for one job in four in 1950; today it accounts for only one in eight, and that share is steadily dropping. Since 1979, the economy has lost three million manufacturing jobs, most of which are not expected to return even with the end of the recession. Moreover, according to research by the economist Barry Bluestone, it is precisely the high-wage sector of the manufacturing economy that is shedding jobs most rapidly.

Other ongoing research by Labor Department economists is comparing prevailing wages in the most rapidly growing occupations with those of occupations in the most rapid decline. This research shows that the twenty fastest-growing jobs pay annual wages that average fully $5,000 *less* than the twenty occupations in steepest decline.

Of course, there is nothing inherent about production work that requires high wages, just as there is nothing inherently low-wage about a service economy. Production work happens to pay well mainly because of the efforts of strong unions. But unions have had little success in organizing secretaries, bank clerks, or even computer assemblers. Moreover, the one sector of the service economy that does pay well—the government—is in decline as a direct employer, for another whole set of historical reasons.

It also happens that the only sector of the manufacturing economy which is growing, microelectronics, shares many of the characteristics of the service economy. Because of its own rapid pace of automation, microelectronics production is not expected to be a mass source of new jobs, good or bad. "High technology," broadly defined, is expected to generate only about 6 percent of the new jobs that the economy will create over the next decade. Moreover, the high-tech field is the quintessential "dual labor market." Its engineers and computer programmers typically have at least one college degree and the prevailing wage is in excess of $30,000 a year. Computer assemblers earn about $6 an hour, far below the prevailing factory wage of over $9. Fewer than one percent of computer assemblers are currently unionized; with unemployment at 10 percent and the electronics industry offering a relatively good set of working conditions and fringe benefits, the microelectronics industry has no trouble recruiting workers, despite the relatively low wage structure.

The high-tech field is also a classic dual labor market in another sense; there is a nearly total absence of career ladders to bridge the gap between the industry's low-skill and high-skill labor forces. There is a thin layer of skilled technicians in between, but it is surprisingly small. The American Electronics Association predicts that the demand for skilled technicians will grow by only about fifteen thousand a year. With close to a million high-wage autoworkers and steelworkers on layoff, those few jobs will not begin to fill the gap.

Despite the vogue for retraining programs, it makes no policy sense to concentrate on the skills of workers when the real problem is the shortage of good jobs. Laid-off autoworkers and steel-workers have been encouraged to enroll in retraining programs, only to find either that no jobs exist at the other end, or that the jobs that are available pay only a fraction of their former wage. Every time openings are announced for jobs that pay more than eight or nine dollars an hour, people begin camping on the sidewalks.

Given these long-term changes in the structure of the economy and the shape of the job market, conventional policy responses are inadequate. The mainstream program to solve unemployment is "economic growth." Growth is, of course, desirable, but if more and more output requires fewer and fewer human workers, and if a growing share of workers producing for American markets are located abroad, then growth by itself won't solve the problem. In theory, all the purchasing power generated by growth "has to go somewhere." But it can go—and is going—to provide jobs overseas, while the jobs that it provides at home are not the kind that a broad middle-class society needs.

The retraining approach is also sadly inadequate. Demand for millions of blue-collar workers with new skills to tend the machines of the high-tech economy simply does not exist. Increasingly, high-tech machines tend themselves. For example, the new field of "Computer-Assisted Design/Computer-Assisted Manufacturing" or CAD/CAM will transform the function of draftsmen. With CAD/CAM, a draftsman turns out blueprints by computer. Several junior colleges have introduced CAD/CAM technician curricula to retrain a generation of draftsmen.

This new career opportunity is, however, likely to be short-lived. Just around the technological corner is something called CIM, which stands for Computer-*Integrated* Manufacturing. With CIM, the engineer who designs a part sits at the computer terminal himself; instead of turning out computer-generated blueprints, CIM transforms the engineer's design directly into parts, and ultimately, products. The "new" job of CAD/CAM technician will go the way of the buggy-whip maker.

By the same token, the usual liberal proposal of massive public works or public employment also fails to solve the problem. For a number of reasons, public works jobs have been short-term and relatively low-paid. Because of the complex relationship between trade unions and the Democratic party, CETA-type programs have been designed not to compete with union labor, or even with non-union full-time career workers. Public works jobs of the usual variety are not likely to replace the disappearing middle of the American labor market or to solve the long-term problem of technological unemployment.

The real solutions to the structural jobs problem, I think, include these:

A coordinated worldwide economic stimulus program, coupled with a managed-trade regime. As the unhappy experience of the first two years of the Mitterrand government showed, Keynesian reflation in one country is just as difficult as "socialism in one country." Our economies today are simply too interdependent to pursue their macroeconomic policies in isolation. If one country reflates by itself, its imports rise, a balance-of-payments crisis occurs, and the attempt at reflation self-destructs.

But even a concerted recovery program does not solve the problem of imports from low-wage areas. To be sure, it is in everyone's interest to help the Third World develop; but there is more than one form of development. It would not be realistic to expect that the welfare states of Europe and North America, whose social contracts are based on decent wages, will permit their own populations to be impoverished as a result of allowing unlimited imports from low-wage countries.

An alternative to a trade free-for-all, in which different nations play by different rules and everyone employs forms of disguised protectionism, is to admit the political nature of the issue and to make the question of where production is located a matter for political bargaining. This sounds like utter heresy, but there are already numerous practical examples.

A good illustration is the trade in textiles. Beginning in the early 1960s, textile imports from low-wage countries were threatening to wipe out the U.S. textile industry. After a series of de facto moves, the United States and Europe eventually negotiated a "Multi-fiber Arrangement"—a frank exception to the General Agreement on Tariff and Trade (GATT) free-trade regime, which recognized that every industrial country wanted to retain a domestic textile industry. Under the multi-fiber agreement, imports of textiles from cheap-labor countries were permitted to grow, but at an annual rate of growth limited to 5 percent. It is worth remembering that textile production, even in the United States, is one of the lowest-wage manufacturing industries, despite a unionization rate of about 20 percent.

Armed with this shield, the American textile industry began to improve its technological advantage. During the 1960s and 1970s, with substantial union cooperation, the domestic manufacturers invested massively in advanced spinning and weaving technology. By 1980, the American industry could boast the world's highest rate of textile productivity. In this case, "protectionism"—far from leading to "subsidized stagnation"—encouraged the textile industry to modernize and stay competitive. And of course it retained jobs for more than a million U.S. workers.

Nor has the multi-fiber arrangement beggared the Third World. Textile exports have continued to grow, and new countries, such as China, have become vigorous competitors. As these newly industrializing nations become more productive, their principal customers will increasingly be their own domestic markets.

Once nations reach approximately the same general wage levels, free trade need not undermine Western living standards and Western social contracts. But as long as the comparative advantage of the newly industrializing countries is based on repression of free trade unions, authoritarian governments working with authoritarian employers, and rock-bottom industrial wages, we have every right to limit imports. Indeed, here is a case for compensating tariffs to be levied on goods from countries that prohibit collective bargaining.

A second illustration is the domestic content legislation sponsored by the United Auto Workers. The bill requires that a substantial proportion of the total value of cars sold in the United States be built with American labor. This approach is far superior to import quotas (the Reagan ad hoc remedy) because it gives the American consumer unlimited access to superior foreign-designed technologies and products and, at the same time, assures that American purchasing power will provide at least some American jobs.

Most studies suggest that the Japanese comparative advantage in automobiles is mainly the result of better management, more efficient use of technology, and superior design—not cheaper labor. Japanese wage rates are lower than American ones, but it takes fewer worker-hours to build a Japanese car. Moreover, only about 24 percent of the cost of building a car is labor cost in any case. Studies have shown that Japanese cars built in America are built with every bit as much labor productivity as those produced in Japan. And whatever advantage does result from cheaper Japanese labor is almost canceled out by shipping costs.

So building Japanese-designed and -capitalized cars in the United States would not exact a hidden tax on American consumers. Quite the contrary; it would benefit the American economy by keeping several hundred thousand high-wage production jobs at home. The domestic content bill is the exact counterpart of the development strategy long used by Japan herself. Before the Japanese Ministry of International Trade and Industry let American semiconductor manufacturers sell their products in Japan, MITI exacted a series of coproduction agreements that served to accelerate the development of Japan's domestic semiconductor industry. More recently, Japan informed Boeing that before Japan Air Lines would order a new generation of planes, Boeing would have to sign an agreement that 15 percent of the added value would be produced in Japan. And the Japanese made sure that the 15 percent represented aeronautical technology that Japan wished to acquire.

Coproduction agreements of this nature, far from restricting world trade, simply change the ground rules. They promote the transfer of technology and, more importantly, assure that products sold in a particular country generate some jobs in that country. This has been the strategy of nations like Brazil with respect to the auto industry for two decades. American and European autoworkers wishing to sell to the big Brazilian consumer market must build auto plants in Brazil. Most European countries rely on similar policies.

The multi-fiber arrangement, by its success in stimulating technological advances, suggests another counter-intuitive conclusion about the relationship of technology to trade: ultimately, *automation* is the solution to a temporary comparative advantage based on cheap labor. If textile production is labor-intensive, and Haitian labor is paid at one-tenth the rate of American labor, the ball game is over unless we are prepared to protect the American domestic market. But what happens when our textile production is heavily automated? Suddenly we can again compete with Haitian textiles on the basis of price and quality, because our capital is more efficient.

The problem, again, is the familiar productivity paradox: automation produces more output at less labor input, and thus makes "everyone" better off—but in the meantime it throws people out of work. When a machine replaces a production worker, both the firm and consumers generally benefit; the loss falls mainly on the worker who loses his job. The "gain" to the firm may be invisible, depending on how competitive the particular industry is. Replacing labor with capital may not increase profits; it may simply permit the firm to hold its own against its competitors, for in a highly competitive industry profits are held down and efficiency gains are passed along to consumers.

If productivity gains are good for the competitiveness of American industry and good for American consumers, but bad for American workers (who are, after all, the same people as consumers except between nine and five), then the $64 billion question is how to socialize productivity gains so that they truly benefit everyone.

As Wassily Leontief has pointed out, failure to redistribute the gains of automation could condemn the society to a paradoxical condition of rising productivity and rising destitution. There has been little practical experimentation with redistribution of work and leisure, especially on this side of the Atlantic; indeed, this is not even a recognized policy issue in the United States.

In Europe, trade unionists have long argued that the solution to technological unemployment is a shorter work week, earlier retirement, pay for longer vacations, and other devices to share available work. The French have applied the boldest version of this program, and it has been only a mixed success. Under the French program, an extra week of vacation was added, the work week is gradually being reduced from forty to thirty-five hours, and firms are encouraged to enter into "solidarity contracts" with their workers and with the state, in which workers agree to take voluntary early retirement and the state bears a substantial share of the cost of supplementary pensions, so that the purchasing power of the retired workers falls only slightly.

This approach has succeeded in stabilizing the unemployment rate at 8–9 percent but has not reduced it much. What might an American version of this approach look like? Here's one variation.

Redistributing productivity gains. Some eleven million Americans are out of work, but millions more are working longer hours than they really want to. Two obvious categories are people over sixty and parents of young children.

The original Social Security Act of 1935 was motivated partly by a desire to make life more comfortable for the elderly; but it was also stimulated by the need to get older people out of the labor force to open up jobs for younger ones. Suppose we adopt a supplemental early retirement incentive program. Unlike Social Security, which is becoming a fiscal drag because it is a pay-as-you-go system, let's prepay our new early retirement program, on the model of an Individual Retirement Account. Call it an ERA, for Early Retirement Account. Under this approach, workers would have a very small deduction taken from their paychecks, which would be matched by the employer and by the government on a one-third/one-third/one-third basis. Eventually, the accumulated capital would be sufficient to permit the worker to drop to a three-day week at age sixty, at full pay. If the average worker earns $12,500 a year, two-fifths of that amount times five years is a comparatively small sum—only $25,000. The payroll deductions necessary to build up to that sum over a thirty-year period, especially given the miracle of compound interest, would be quite trivial—less than $200 a year. This system would also help the national savings rate, a favorite cause of capital-conscious conservatives. But it would do so without further enriching the rich. By enticing millions of workers over sixty to take life a little easier (but to continue productive work), this would open up millions of jobs for younger workers.

As the parent of two school-age children, I propose working parents in the two-income family as my other nominees for oppressed workers. In theory, feminism and the family with two working parents was not just supposed to give women a ticket of entry to the male rat race; they were also supposed to allow men the luxury of some female values—nurturing, caregiving, and so forth. Remember? But things haven't worked out quite that way. Despite the entry of millions of women into the labor force, wage cuts have outpaced the additional income brought into the family by working women. Average household income has actually fallen by 11 percent since 1973. The average woman with a full-time job outside the home still spends thirty hours a week on housework, according the Labor Department. And very, very few fathers have taken advantage of working spouses in order to spend more time at home. Neither the drop in family income nor the conventional structure of career ladders permits it.

A proposal: Every parent, male and female, living with a minor child shall be entitled to five years of full-time pay for half-time work. The benefit would be capped at, say, 100 percent of the first $12,000 of income, and 70 percent of the next $12,000, so that millionaires could not drop to half-time work at government subsidy.

This would accomplish two things. It would be good social policy in its own right. Parents would be able to be less frantically job-obsessed during the years when their children need them most. In the case of two-parent households, there could be a total of ten years when at least one parent was in the home at least half time. In the case of a one-parent family, this would provide a far superior alternative to welfare. Secondly, of course, this particular form of family allowance would serve to free millions of person-years of jobs for people who are now unemployed. It would be a way of sharing available work in a manner that also served the critical social goal of shoring up family life.

As the economy becomes more and more productive, and as

fewer and fewer workers are needed to produce society's material goods, other variations could be added, like periodic paid sabbaticals for everyone in the workforce. The frequency, duration, and timing of these could be adjusted periodically, to provide a fine-tuning device for maintaining full employment.

There is one caveat to this approach. In macro-economic terms, a transfer is a transfer is a transfer. Somewhere, the money must exist to finance these new income transfers; otherwise, we are simply reallocating an inadequate supply of real income; income will be more equitably shared, but we will lack the money to maintain full-time living standards for part-time work. To some degree, of course, this system packs a Keynesian punch. To the extent that it reallocates purchasing power and reduces involuntary unemployment, it stimulates aggregate demand, which in turn stimulates the growth necessary to provide the real resources to finance the program. While it is unlikely that we will experience enough productivity growth to rely solely on work-sharing to solve the unemployment problem, it is nonetheless an indispensable part of an overall program.

Procurement as industrial policy. Even more fundamental than work-sharing is the need to maximize total output as fewer and fewer workers are needed for production of physical goods. Obviously, a full-employment commitment is the beginning and end of any progressive economic program. Without full employment, workers who do have jobs lose their bargaining power to demand fair wages, and the state incurs the cost of supporting all those who have lost jobs. Neither make-work nor share-work, by themselves, get the society to full employment with maximized output. We also need to devise a means to redistribute some of the increased purchasing power that results from productivity gains—and turn it into both good jobs and the production of socially desired goods and services. In other words, the state has to devise a way to create the effective demand for commodities and services that have "use-values," but for which the private market does not generate effective purchasing power.

There is a well-proven American model for accomplishing this redistribution and translation of purchasing power into jobs.

It is, unfortunately, the Pentagon. To a lesser degree, it is also NASA.

Consider the World War II experience. During World War II, the U.S. government mobilized more purchasing power than the country had ever seen. During the first six months of 1942, the War Department entered more orders than the entire value of the Gross National Product of 1940! By 1944, the peak year of war production, the Keynesian prod of war production had so stimulated the economy as a whole that *civilian* output alone exceeded the economy's entire output of 1940. And we accomplished that, even though half of what we produced was made in order to be blown up. During the war, GNP expanded at an unheard-of rate of 13 percent per year. Today, we are congratulating ourselves that the 1983 "recovery" temporarily attained a growth rate of 5 percent, and economists debate whether such a rate can be sustained.

World War II was also a formidable human capital policy. People with no prior experience in factories came off the farms to take good jobs in war plants. Women also learned blue-collar production jobs. During the war we trained 300,000 skilled machinists, a training feat that has never been equaled. The United States is now facing a shortage of experienced "A" machinists, in large part because about two-thirds of the senior machinists all reached retirement age about the same time—forty years after World War II!

For thirty years, it has been fashionable in conservative circles to aver that "it wasn't the New Deal that cured the Great Depression; it was the war." True enough. But anybody who thinks that World War II was anything other than a massive dose of Keynesian demand stimulus is kidding himself and the public. The supply-side nostrums—subsidizing the cost of capital and lowering the taxes to be paid on anticipated profits—may stimulate some new productive investment (*if* the entrepreneur is reasonably sure of a market for the product). But a government contract—a guarantee to purchase what is produced—is what really works miracles. If American industry can actually design and produce *guided missiles on railroad tracks* for the sole reason that the United States government is willing to write a check to pay for them, it is safe to assume that American industry can produce almost anything.

War production generates a Keynesian "big bang" in several complementary respects. It puts the unemployed back to work, and at relatively high-paid jobs. Whether production is accomplished in the public sector or through contracts with privately owned industry is optional; it accomplishes the same Keynesian jolt to aggregate purchasing power. During World War II, a good deal of the research and development was public (or under contract to universities); much of the production was private. But there was a substantial degree of planning and coordination by the government. Not only does a World War II–style jump in public procurement put people back to work, train them at high skills, and boost purchasing power generally; it also sets in motion a technological dynamism. We are still living off many of the technological advances seeded by World War II defense contracting—synthetic rubber, the transistor, early computer science, America's early lead in civil aviation, and of course (for better or worse), atomic energy.

Moreover, procurement contracts do not just allow industry to make profits and hire workers by meeting current orders; they also subsidize the rebuilding and improvement of capital equipment. The civil aircraft and the automobiles and the chemical fertilizer industry that roared into full production to meet the postwar demands of returning veterans and their families were not produced by plants and machines that had to be built from scratch. They were built in converted war production plants. Tank lines became car lines; ordnance production became chemical fertilizer production.

The World War II example immediately throws into relief the fallacy of the conservative claim that government allocation of capital must necessarily retard output because it deploys capital "less optimally" than the market. When output expands at 13 percent a year, the economy can afford a lot of suboptimal use of capital! Conversely, when eleven million people are out of work and industry is producing at below 70 percent of capacity, the genius of the market for allocating capital isn't worth very much.

It is axiomatic that government procurement wastes some money. But idle resources waste more money. Keynes himself, in a celebrated passage, observed that if the government buried old banknotes in bottles and paid jobless workers to dig them up, it would be preferable to keeping them idle. In a sense, paying workers to build the implements of war is tantamount to paying them to dig up old bottles. Neither process produces useful goods for the domestic civilian economy. Defense production, however, has a patriotic aura about it, which imparts to it all sorts of virtues that enable conservatives to overlook the intimate involvement of the government.

The challenge, therefore, is to find civilian economic counterparts to World War II. The closest thing to a "civilian Pentagon" proposal in the political mainstream is Senator Kennedy's call for a domestic technology agency, which would award contracts to private industry. Unlike Pentagon contracts, the purpose of these projects would be to stimulate the development of technologies and products with civilian applications.

One could go a big step further and create an agency that would enter into contracts whose purpose is not just the development of technology, but the creation of useful goods and services and the redevelopment of regional economies suffering high unemployment. If America could grow at a rate of 13 percent a year on war production (much of which was blown up), just imagine how fast we could grow if the output went for useful goods and services. Suppose the government offered to buy a minicomputer for every classroom in America, subject only to the proviso that all of the production be carried out domestically. Suppose the government guaranteed a public school teacher-pupil ratio of one to fifteen. Suppose the government determined to replace every subway car older than ten years. Suppose the government pledged to finance the development of a commercially viable system of decentralized photoelectric domestic power generation.

Make up your own wish list of socially useful products that

provide jobs. If employing people to build bombs and guns and planes to blow up half of Europe could energize a rapid economic recovery, production of *anything* can energize a recovery. A civilian economic equivalent of World War II has other advantages. It is far less inflationary than a war. In war, much of the added production goes up in smoke. In the civilian equivalent a government contract translates into useful products, so there is less of a problem of too much demand chasing too little supply. Government procurement is also an excellent planning tool. The procurement can be targeted in areas of high unemployment, or to particular industries, or to create new forms of ownership.

Unfortunately, "industrial policy" has been defined largely as the subsidy or provision of *capital*, not of production. For most of its advocates, industrial policy turns out to mean, in practice, some form of development bank or equity capital agency. That is far too limiting, and also too accepting of supply-side assumptions. Subsidizing capital accomplishes little when there is no assurance of a market for the product. Government procurement, in contrast, *creates* the market. It tells the contractor exactly what to produce, but leaves it to the contractor's ingenuity to figure out *how* to produce it. Anybody who thinks this inevitably leads to lemon products has never flown in an F-15. Government contracting has created technological marvels. Unfortunately, most have been in the military sector, which is almost totally isolated from the discipline of consumer markets. But it is also possible to deploy government contracts creatively to energize new, dynamic civilian sectors—and not just by buying new generations of products. The Japanese, shrewdly, create markets for new generations of capital goods by offering to buy out old capital goods.

All of this, to be sure, will require the expenditure of tax dollars and, in the short run, will increase public deficits. But the surest way—and, in the long run, the only way—to bring deficits back to moderate proportions is to get the economy back to full employment. Deficits that reflect high unemployment and shrunken tax bases create a self-perpetuating recession that will never cure either itself or the deficits it perpetuates.

Active labor market policies. Retraining, by itself, is no remedy for 10 percent unemployment. But coupled with a commitment to full employment as a fundamental policy goal, active labor market policies are very useful. The Swedes have devised a system of local labor market boards, which report to a national labor market board (the AMS). Under this system, workers are encouraged to take advantage of retraining opportunities—not just to upgrade the quality of the workforce as a whole, to ease inflationary shortages of skilled workers, and to match manpower supply to manpower demand, but also to take up slack during periods of high unemployment. At peak periods of joblessness, as much as 5 percent of the entire Swedish labor force is in some training program under the sponsorship of a labor market board. Translated into American proportions, this would equal over five million people.

If we are serious about an industrial policy and a commitment to full employment, an entirely different approach to retraining is required. One promising variation is the use of retraining vouchers; another is wage subsidy vouchers. Under this approach, any worker laid off because of technological advances would be given a voucher that was worth, say, half of five years' pay to that worker's next employer. By subsidizing wages directly (rather than through tax gimmickry), this approach would send the dislocated worker to the head of the job line. It would also give a needed competitive advantage to cities and towns hard hit by plant relocations. In a Youngstown or a Flint, a prospective new employer would find thousands of skilled workers, all holding job vouchers that would add up to a subsidy of half of the employer's labor costs for five years.

At present, American labor market policy consists mainly of paying unemployment compensation to the unemployed, on the assumption that their joblessness is temporary. We also have a parallel system of paying means-tested (welfare) subsistence benefits to the jobless who do not have a history of gainful employment or an ability to take full-time work. All of this income transfer represents a resource that could be used for retraining and for wage subsidies, rather than simply for subsistence.

Don't mourn, organize. The single most important piece of

public policy that supported the postwar, high-wage social contract was not job retraining through CETA, or even minimum wage legislation. It was the Wagner Act.

As the American workforce is radically transformed in response to changes in the mobility of capital and the technology of industry, a strong labor movement is crucial to defend decent wages, to negotiate these transformations so that they are not paid for only by workers, and to provide a long-term constituency for progressive policies generally. The present labor movement surely has its flaws, but a look at the sweep of progressive legislation over the past forty years suggests that the labor movement is, if not the only game in town, the indispensable ally for the other enterprises—the civil rights, environmental, consumerist, feminist, and other progressive movements.

During the past ten years, the postwar consensus in which big corporations grudgingly tolerated labor organization has been unilaterally abrogated by management. It is now open season on labor unions. The nearly fifty-year-old structure of labor law is in desperate need of overhaul. Government should once again be the ally of labor organizing that it was during the New Deal, and labor unions themselves should be encouraged to take on the new issues of work quality, work organization, and the influence of technology on work, as well as that most "un-American" labor issue of all: how capital is to be invested, and for what.

III. WOMEN AND THE WELFARE STATE

BARBARA EHRENREICH *and* FRANCES FOX PIVEN

To judge from the Democratic party's response to three years of budget cuts, liberalism is as dead as chivalry. While the Reagan administration savaged social programs that served primarily women and children, most congressional Democrats simply shrugged and stood aside. The party that had once been proud to claim the New Deal and the Great Society seemed almost abashed by its own past accomplishments, ready to accept the Republican judgment that social spending is a luxury the United States can no longer afford. The poor were deserted by their traditional advocates when they needed them most. But the poor have found new allies, and this is likely to be one of the most important political developments of the eighties. Where conventional liberalism fears to tread, feminism is moving in.

The groups taking up the defense of social welfare programs in Washington today include not only the National Organization for Women (NOW) and the NAACP, which have always been on the liberal side, but a surprising range of organizations representing women's interests. The usually staid League of Women Voters and the American Nurses' Association are among the new groups a congressman can expect to run afoul of when he votes down social welfare spending. In 1982, over fifty national organizations—mostly women's organizations, such as the National Council of Jewish Women, National Institute for Women of Color, and Rural American Women—issued a collective indictment of the administration entitled "Inequality of Sacrifice." The message was simple: the poor in America, who have long been disproportionately black, are now disproportionately female, so that policies that hurt the poor hurt, above all, women and their dependent children. Among the feminists who, as the right suspects, populate mainstream women's organizations, the logic is taken one step further: policies that hurt some women, potentially hurt all women.

The defense of the welfare state is no easy task at a time when leaders of both parties are blasting the evils of "big government," and when even many on the left associate social welfare programs with an unhealthy dependency. What is required is a feminist perspective on the contemporary American economy, and the role of social welfare programs in that economy, that counters the laissez faire arguments of the Republican right.

THE FEMINIST DEMAND FOR GOVERNMENT INTERVENTION

From the time of its emergence in the mid-nineteenth century, the organized women's movement has found itself pitted against the doctrines of American laissez faire. Women fought for government regulations to curb alcohol, gambling, and prostitution; for legislation to protect children and women from wanton exploitation in the labor market; for urban public health measures, day care centers, and widows' pensions to ease the lives of impoverished women. And when their efforts in state and local politics failed, crusading women sometimes, as in their struggle for child labor legislation, turned to the national government for the policies that would override local opposition.

Contemporary feminists are often hesitant to claim this heritage of women's activism. The women reformers of the late nineteenth and early twentieth centuries, including those who considered themselves feminists, were middle-class and upper-class, and their politics were often colored by antipathies to the poorer people they sought to "uplift." Moreover, even as these women entered the public world of politics, they did so to assert the sanctity of motherhood and family life, values we associate with the sentimentalism of Victorian culture and the extreme subordination of women in Victorian society.

But the feminist reformers of the late nineteenth century did not merely reflect the biases of their time and class, nor were they merely sentimentalists who accepted the subordination of women. Their commitment to "home values" generated singular beliefs about how society should be organized—beliefs different from, and in some ways a challenge to, the dominant credo of a burgeoning market economy. As Dolores Hayden concludes, most feminists wanted to increase women's rights within the home and "simultaneously bring homelike nurturing into public life"; or, in the words of Frances Willard, leader of the Women's Christian Temperance Union, to "bring the home into the world." In the process of what they saw as an effort to bring the caretaking values of motherhood into public life, they worked and fought for very material and practical reforms to protect poor and working women and children.

A good many women reformers came to see an enlarged role for government as the main hope for sustaining the values of security and nurturance against the assaults of an expanding market economy. It was out of such commitments that some notable feminist leaders, such as Charlotte Perkins Gilman, came to take up the cause of American socialism, which they found compelling for the promise it offered of economic security through a planned economy. But even when they did not turn to socialism, they turned to government. "The new truth, electrifying, glorifying American womanhood today," declared suffragist Elizabeth Boynton Harbert in 1878, "is the discovery that the State is but the larger family, the nation the old homestead, and that in this national home there is a room and a corner and a duty for 'mother.'" At a time when the dominant view was that government must be limited in order to guarantee liberty and prosperity, this was an extraordinary idea.

At first glance, the developing clash between women and the Republican right seems to be only a continuation of this historical conflict over the role of government. On the one side, the Reagan administration waves the old banner of laissez faire to justify deregulation and the destruction of social programs. On the other side, women—with their historic commitment to economic security and their longstanding disadvantage in the marketplace—are squaring off in opposition. Most Americans now share the historic feminist conviction that government has at least some responsibility for the nation's economic well-being. This is due mostly to the fact that laissez-faire ideas no longer describe the workings of the economy, and, indeed, no longer even conform to the needs of private business. A vastly expanded government has come to play a major role in the economy. It is not an overstatement to say that the United States is now as much a *public economy* as a market economy.

THE EMERGENCE OF
THE WELFARE STATE

Contemporary conservatives attribute public pressure for expansion of social welfare programs to a misplaced sense of entitlement. It might more reasonably be understood as a correct assessment of the actual role of government. As government support of private business grew, the aspects of American economic activity that could credibly be construed as simply market activities commensurately shrank, and the groundwork was laid for profound changes in the public perception of the relationship between economic and political life. In the place of nineteenth-century laissez faire ideas, new beliefs began to emerge: a conviction that political rights, particularly the right to participate in government, should be exercised to protect the economic well-being of ordinary people. In the twentieth century, movements of the poor and the unemployed, of workers and the aged took up the cause of economic security. Their struggles bore fruit in the American welfare state.

The first social welfare programs on a national scale were established during the Great Depression. A huge temporary relief program was created, followed soon after by the Social Security Act, which established the legislative framework for our most important programs for the aged and disabled, the unemployed, and impoverished mothers and their children. Some three decades later, another wave of economic protests, this time mostly by blacks, led to the expansion of these early programs and the addition of significant new programs in health care, housing, and nutrition.

WOMEN'S STAKE IN SOCIAL WELFARE

Today, it is women—and their dependent children—who are the primary beneficiaries of social welfare programs for the poor. The reason for this is that, overall, women's economic status has deteriorated, and most markedly in the 1970s. Between the mid-sixties and mid-seventies, the number of poor adult males declined, while the number of the poor in households headed by women swelled by 100,000 a year. By 1980, the American poor were predominantly female; two out of three adults whose income fell below the official federal poverty line were women, and more than half the families who were poor were headed by women. This trend prompted the National Advisory Council on Economic Opportunity (since disbanded by the Reagan administration) to observe that "all other things being equal, if the proportion of poor in female-householder families were to continue to increase at the same rate as it did from 1967 to 1978, the poverty population would be composed solely of women and their children before the year 2000." Poverty in the United States has always been disproportionately concentrated among minorities, but this convergence of gender and class is unprecedented in American history.

The causes for the feminization of poverty are rooted in profound changes in American society. Like most industrialized capitalist countries, we have long presumed a "family wage" system. The achievement of a family wage for men, meaning earnings sufficient to support a wife and children, was an important victory of the late nineteenth- and early twentieth-century labor struggles. But this achievement by unionized male workers helped to thwart women's aspirations for higher wages, particularly in typically female occupations. Of course, not all men, and certainly not all black men, earned enough to support families, nor were all women supported by men. Nevertheless, the assumption that women entered the workforce only as secondary workers reinforced the segregation of women into low paying occupations and legitimated systematic wage discrimination against women. For those women who could depend on the earnings of a male breadwinner, however, the system did offer economic security, if not the dignity of economic independence.

In the course of only two decades, the family wage system has ceased to provide economic security for women and their children. Increasingly, women must depend on their own earnings, and even when they do not, they can't count as they once did on the earnings of men. Yet the assumption of the family wage system remains firmly embedded in a wage structure that offers women, hour for hour, only 60 percent of the average male wage. What is usually called "the breakdown of the family" occurred without equalizing changes in the labor market, and this accounts for the disproportionate impoverishment of women.

For many women, poverty begins when their marriages end. Half of the marriages in the United States now end in divorce, and 80 percent of the children of divorced parents remain with their mothers. Child support payments are a negligible source of income for most of these families. Forty percent of divorced fathers contribute nothing, and those who do contribute pay, on the average, less than $2,100 a year. Many other women are poor before they become mothers, and for them, having the sole responsibility for their children is only another barrier to achieving economic self-sufficiency in the labor market.

Women who both raise and support their children need, of

course, to earn a "family wage," just as many married women also need to earn a substantial portion of their families' income. Yet the median annual income for working women is $11,591 a year, while, according to the Bureau of Labor Statistics, a family of four now requires $25,000 a year to maintain an "intermediate" standard of living. The primary reason for the low earnings of women is occupational segregation. The overwhelming majority (80 percent) of jobs held by women are concentrated in only 20 of 420 occupations listed by the Department of Labor. These occupations are mainly in retail sales, clerical work, light assembly, and the catchall category of "service work," and they are characteristically low-paid and dead-ended. In fact, real earnings have been declining in the sectors of the workforce in which women are concentrated. Between 1973 and 1979, average hourly earnings in services, measured in 1972 dollars, fell from $3.16 to $3.08; earnings in retail trade fell from $2.70 to $2.61. In the same period, earnings in largely male manufacturing jobs increased.

As a result of the combined effects of changes in family patterns and occupational segregation, the fastest-growing group among the female poor are single mothers with young children. By 1981, the census reported 9.4 million female heads of families. (Meanwhile, the media's fancy notwithstanding, the number of men raising children on their own showed no significant increase in the decade of the seventies.) The increase in households headed by women is most striking among blacks, and 46.8 percent of black families are now female-headed, as compared to 13.4 percent of white families. But despite the stereotype of the "black welfare mothers," poor female-headed households are now increasing more rapidly among whites than among blacks.

What are the chances for progress out of the occupational ghetto of "women's work"? Some trends are encouraging. Where only 4 percent of the nation's lawyers and judges were women in 1971, women accounted for 14 percent in 1981. In the same period, the precentage of the nation's physicians who are women rose from 9 to 22 percent, the percentage of female engineers increased fourfold (from 1 percent to 4 percent), and the number of women holding skilled blue-collar jobs also increased. But despite these gains by a narrow stratum of better-prepared women, average female earnings relative to men actually sank slightly—depressing evidence of the deterioration of the economic status of the majority of women workers.

Long-term structural trends within the United States economy offer little hope that market forces will produce an upturn in the occupational prospects of women. This is not because the number of jobs available to women is declining. In fact, low-paid "women's work" is expanding, because of two important trends in the labor market. One is the long-term sectoral shift away from manufacturing and toward service and clerical jobs. In the 1970s this shift accelerated, as a result both of expansion in the service and retail sectors and a rapid decline in manufacturing, especially in the highly unionized and well-paid steel, automobile, and rubber industries. According to Emma Rothschild, 70 percent of all new private-sector jobs created between 1973 and 1980 were stereotypically women's jobs, in such areas as fast foods, data processing and other business services, and health care. The result is a marked feminization of the workforce, but in jobs that are "badly paid, unchanging and economically unproductive."

A second trend affecting both the gender composition of the workforce and women's economic status is the reorganization of work associated with increasing automation. In his classic 1974 study, *Labor and Monopoly Capital*, Harry Braverman showed that the pressure to maximize profits leads employers to replace well-paid, skilled jobs with badly paid, unskilled jobs that are likely to be defined as "women's work." Automation, and most spectacularly the automation made possible by new microelectronic technology, accelerates this trend toward what Braverman calls "the degradation of labor." Skilled jobs for men become less skilled jobs for women, and skilled work for women is replaced by less skilled work: the machinist is replaced by an unskilled operator; the department store buyer by the clerk who tends a computerized inventory system; the secretary by the word processor operator.

In short, the occupational ghetto of "women's work" has enlarged, and opportunities for both men and women outside that ghetto have shrunk. One obvious consequence is that fewer men will be able to earn a family wage—a fact that renders the antifeminist ideal of the restored family with a male bread-winner and female housewife utterly hollow. More and more women, married or not, will have no choice but to be wage earners. Another consequence is that many women will be poor whether or not they are employed.

WOMEN AND SOCIAL WELFARE PROGRAMS

In a hostile economy, women—and not only poor women—have come to rely more and more on government social welfare programs for their economic security. In part this results from women's greater longevity, which enables women to benefit disproportionately from programs where eligibility is determined mainly by age. Thus women receive 54 percent of Social Security benefits, despite the fact that the average benefit paid to women is almost one-third lower than that paid to men ($215.80 a month compared to $308.70). Similarly, almost 60 percent of those covered by Medicare are women. Flawed though these programs may be, they are critical to the survival of a majority of older women who would otherwise be desperately poor.

Other programs are not age-tested but "means-tested": eligibility is conditional on poverty. The reliance of women on these programs has risen apace with the increase of poverty among women. In particular, female-headed families have come to rely heavily on government social welfare programs. In 1979, over 3.3 million of these families, or 34.6 percent of the total number of female-headed families, received funds from Aid to Families with Dependent Children (AFDC), according to the Census Bureau; an almost equal number were covered by Medicaid; 2.6 million were enrolled in the Food Stamp program; and 2.3 percent were enrolled in the school lunch program. Thus government social welfare benefits have reduced some of the income gap suffered by the families headed by women who can no longer rely on a male wage. In other words, the breakdown of a system of intrafamily income transfers from husband to wife has been partially offset by the expansion of a system of public income transfers.

A second group of women who benefit from government social welfare programs are those in the expanding low-wage service and clerical sectors of the workforce. For these women, social welfare programs provide some protection against employer abuses, whether low wages, unpaid overtime work, speed-ups, or personal and sexual harassment. It is easier for a woman to resist unfair demands and risk being fired when she knows that the result will not be starvation for herself and her children. Furthermore, because social welfare benefits reduce desperation among the unemployed, the latter are less likely to undercut the wages and working conditions of those who do have jobs. By reducing economic insecurity, the social programs thus enhance the workplace power of millions of low-wage working women.

The third group of women whose livelihood depends on social welfare programs are those who are employed by them. In 1980, fully 70 percent of the 17.3 million social service jobs on all levels of government (including education) were held by women. These jobs accounted for fully a quarter of all female employment, according to Massachusetts Institute of Technology professors Lisa Peattie and Martin Rein, and for about half of professional jobs held by women. As the Reagan administration presses for a shift of funds from social welfare to military spending, many of these jobs will be lost, and there will be no compensatory employment gains for women. Only 0.5 percent of the entire female workforce is engaged in work on military contracts. A study by Employment Research Associates estimates that with each $1 billion increase in the military budget, 9,500 jobs are lost to women in social welfare or the private sector.

ACCOMPLISHMENTS AND FAILURES

The achievements of America's federally sponsored welfare programs are obvious, especially for women, but not only for women. Social Security provides some guarantees against the terrors of a poverty-stricken old age for the millions of Americans who have no private pensions or whose pensions fall woefully short of a subsistence income. Medicaid and Medicare make it possible for more millions of both the elderly and the poor—who are, of course, the groups most likely to suffer from chronic disease and disabilities—to receive the medical attention previously largely unavailable to them. Unemployment insurance reduces some of the fear of joblessness for most of the middle class as well as the poor, and helps tide those actually out of work over the dislocations caused by cyclical downturns and shifting patterns of investment. Federal disability programs make the fate of the ill and the crippled less miserable. Nutritional programs, particularly Food Stamps and supplements for women and infants, are credited with significantly reducing hunger and the most common forms of malnutrition. And Aid to Families with Dependent Children provides at least a meager subsistence to millions of the most desperately impoverished mothers and their children. All told, an estimated one-third of Americans now depend to some degree on government social welfare programs.

In addition to easing the economic insecurity of millions of Americans, federally funded social welfare programs have often made possible innovative services and new opportunities for citizen participation. In a number of the Great Society programs of the 1960s, the federal government effectively bypassed entrenched local political hierarchies and called for "maximum feasible participation" of the communities served. People who had never before had a role in public decision-making gained positions on the federally mandated community advisory boards of health, mental health, and multi-service centers, giving the recipients of services, for the first time, a voice in determining what their needs were and how they might best be met. Similarly, federal funding for rape crisis centers and battered women's refuges bypassed local male politicians and gave women, many of them feminist activists, a chance to create client-centered services sensitive to women's needs. Republican hostility to these programs stems, in no small part, from their role in the political empowerment of women, minorities, and the poor.

Despite these achievements, however, there is no question but that the social welfare programs established in response to the upheavals of the 1930s and 1960s are flawed and imperfect. The loudest critics today are on the Republican right. For nearly two decades, however, it was those who actually depended on the programs—including client groups and their advocates, women's organizations, and labor unions—who were sharply critical. On the surface it seems that no one, either right or left, supports the social welfare programs, and this helps account for the timid response that has been made to the Reagan administration's cuts.

In fact, however, very different sorts of criticisms are at issue. The right attacks the programs for their high cost and their allegedly corrosive effect on the incentive to work. By contrast, the left criticizes the programs for bureaucratic indifference to clients; for the low level of benefits or services; for the punitive terms often exacted as a condition for receiving benefits or services; and for profiteering by businesses involved in the provision of services. Not only is this a different critique from that made by the right; it is in fact an opposing critique, and it stems from an opposite assessment of the responsibility of government.

In the most important sense, the shortcomings of American social welfare result from the complex political forces that shaped the original programs and continue to reshape them over time. Demands by the unemployed or the poor or the aged were resisted by employer interests, who feared that if government provided subsistence to large numbers of people, labor markets would be weakened. As a result, the benefit levels of the key income maintenance programs, including unemployment insurance and AFDC, have always been very low. Other programs, particularly those that provided "in-kind" benefits in the form of food subsidies or housing, or those that provided services like medical care, easily became the target of lobbyists who stood to profit from taking over the provision of benefits or services.

Business pressures also explain why a number of the most important programs were not federally based but left to state (and sometimes local) governments to administer. For reasons that are hardly mysterious, business interests have always exerted great influence on state and local programs. When businessmen demand low taxes and restrictive social programs at the state or local level, they wield the threat of relocation. Moreover, because business interests can successfully resist state and local taxes, the revenues to fund programs at the state and local level must be exacted by means of regressive taxes on working people. This pattern in turn generates a climate of resentment and hostility toward locally financed programs for the poor. As a consequence, benefit levels set by the states have been kept well below the lowest local wage rates. In addition, programs have been thoroughly encased in an elaborate bureaucratic apparatus of procedures and conditions so that as little aid as possible would be given to as few as possible. Finally, the degrading treatment of those who survived the bureaucratic runarounds ensured that few would choose welfare who could survive otherwise.

The AFDC and Medicaid programs illustrate the deforming effects of private business interests on American social welfare. AFDC is notorious for its humiliating treatment of clients and the inadequacy of the benefits it provides. Monthly payments to a family of three averaged slightly under $300 in 1980, and only nine states provide more than $400 a month. In no state is the combination of AFDC and Food Stamps sufficient to raise a family *up to* the official poverty line. AFDC originated as a program of cash benefits to impoverished mothers raising children without a male breadwinner, and it reflected the recognition that such women cannot be expected to support their children by their own efforts. That recognition, however, has always been at war with another, usually unstated, imperative— that government not provide benefits that compete with low-wage work. Thus, although AFDC is the only program that attempts to meet the daily needs of poor children, it is pegged far below the poverty level in order, ultimately, to avoid any challenge to the determination of wages by market forces.

The gratuitous humiliation inflicted upon clients by welfare bureaucracies reinforces this effect, for it works to ensure that few will choose welfare over work, no matter what the terms. Of course, abysmal poverty and degrading treatment have other effects: depressing the expectations of poor women and their children, destroying their morale, and making certain that they do not come to believe they have legitimate rights, even to a subsistence income. In this way, AFDC helps to create the very caricature of the demoralized and dependent recipient that is then used to justify the harshness of the program.

The Medicaid program illustrates different flaws resulting from the influence of different market interests. For decades before Medicaid and Medicare were legislated, private interests in the health sector, particularly the American Medical Association (AMA) and the insurance industry, had fiercely and successfully resisted any major program of government health insurance. Medicaid and Medicare were passed only over the bitter resistance of the AMA, and then only in a form that ensured that the new government financing mechanisms would not affect private control of the organization and delivery of medical care. From the inception of these programs in 1966, health reformers criticized them as inadequate and patchwork substitutes for a national health service that would guarantee the actual delivery of high-quality care. Even so, reform groups expected that Medicaid would make health care financially accessible to many of the nation's "medically indigent" (people who, while not classified as poor, nevertheless cannot afford medical care).

While Medicaid helped many of the nation's poor to gain access to medical attention, the program had other, unexpectedly perverse, effects. Medicaid, combined with Medicare, contributed to the rapid and still escalating costs of medical care. Conservative critics argue that this is the result of the excessive consumption of health services by the poor and elderly, and that prices have risen with increased demand. The health system, however, is notoriously impervious to ordinary laws of supply and demand. It is mainly doctors who determine the demand for health services; only they can decide whether a problem will be dealt with in one visit or through extensive diagnostic and treatment procedures. Moreover, provider groups such as the American Medical Association and the American Hospital Association have lobbied hard, and largely successfully, to minimize government control of the prices of their services. As a consequence, these programs have turned out to be a bonanza for the medical industry. For everyone else, especially the over 30 million people who presently lack coverage of any kind, it has meant spiraling medical costs and reduced access to care.

Like AFDC, Medicaid is administered and partly financed by the states, and benefits and eligibility have largely been left to the discretion of individual states. The states have set eligibility levels so low that most of the people the program was originally intended to serve have been excluded. In fact, in almost all states, Medicaid eligibility is tied to welfare eligibility. Strained state budgets, combined with the identification of Medicaid as a "welfare program," made it an easy target for budget cutters. Consequently, as medical inflation encouraged by some features of the program has driven costs up, Medicaid coverage has shrunk, providing fewer services to proportionately fewer of the people who need care.

None of these failures was the result of the inevitable bumbling of "big government." Rather, they were the result of a weak government—a government so weak it ceded administrative control over many of the programs to states and localities where they were cannibalized by hostile interests, so weak it could not establish decent benefit levels, so weak it could not curb the distortions forced on it by private market interests. A weak government has produced weak programs, and weak programs are indeed difficult to defend.

The right-wing critique of the welfare state pointed to a clear direction for the reorganization and contraction of the programs the Reagan administration has attempted to implement. Underlying each of its major initiatives was an effort not only to slash benefits and services, but to increase the power of business interests and reduce the power of beneficiary groups. This was the significance of the administration's "new federalism" proposals, which would have entirely abdicated the federal role in the AFDC or the Food Stamp program in favor of state and local government. The administration's persisting efforts to eliminate the legal services program and to rewrite the regulations of a number of the programs so as to weaken procedural safeguards are similarly an effort to shift power relations by expunging the legal rights of program beneficiaries.

But if the critique of the welfare state from the right pointed the direction for concrete changes, so does the critique developed by left and liberal reformers. In fact, the specific elements of an expanded and reformed social welfare policy have been outlined before, by the Welfare Rights Movement in the 1960s and by the feminist movement in the 1970s. Our agenda should begin, very simply, with the demand for higher levels of benefits. Nothing could be more critical to the well-being of poor women and children than an immediate increase in the benefit levels of the AFDC program, for example, which, at a minimum, should support families at a level well above what is officially defined as "poverty."

Beyond this obvious shorter-term goal, we should begin to work for organizational reforms that will strengthen the influence of the beneficiaries of income maintenance programs and reduce the influence of business. Three basic principles can guide us. First, responsibility for social welfare programs should be firmly fixed at the federal level. Influence from the right works for decentralization to the state level in order to increase the power of business interests over the income maintenance programs that bear most directly on labor markets. For just this reason, we should fight for the outright nationalization of financing and policy-making responsibility in programs such as AFDC, unemployment insurance, and Medicaid. Benefits and eligibility standards should be uniform across the nation, and their financing should not be subject to the whims of state legislators.

Second, bureaucratic discretion in the determination of eligibility and benefits should be limited. Notwithstanding its avowed hostility to "government interference," the right has worked to increase bureaucratic discretion and to strip beneficiaries of procedural protections. Arbitrary and variable decisions can be shattering to recipients and reinforce the notion that social welfare programs are a form of charity. It follows that we should work for the elimination of elaborate conditions for determining eligibility—conditions that inevitably increase bureaucratic discretion and intimidate applicants. In their stead, we should promote broad and easily determined criteria that reduce the need for invasive investigation and give benefits and services the status of *legal rights*.

And third, over the longer term, we should work toward the consolidation of programs so as to promote common stakes and stronger alliances among the many segments of the American population that have come to rely upon the welfare state. The present system separates means-tested programs such as Medicaid from universal programs such as Medicare and Social Security, thus breeding competition and animosity among recipient groups. Worse, within these broad categories, an incredible array of disparate programs apply differently to people depending on their age, their sex, their marital status, the specifics of their former employment, or even on the value of their home furnishings. The right has capitalized on the fragmentation of social welfare programs and their recipients. It follows that we should work for a unified system which, through the breadth and strength of its constituency, would not be vulnerable to attack by a business-oriented President or Congress.

An adequate and unified system of income maintenance would go a long way toward easing the economic insecurity of low-paid working women as well as improving the lives of women already in poverty. But an income support program cannot provide goods and services if these are not available in the market at affordable prices. Private business has not found it profitable to operate child care centers or clinics offering primary and preventive health care in low-income areas, much less centers for rape victims or refuges for battered women. And market-priced housing will also remain beyond the reach of most women, even if the income programs are improved.

Of all these services, perhaps none is more critical to women than child care. It seems obvious to us that, without affordable and reliable child care options, mothers of young children should not be expected to enter the labor market or job training programs. Yet many women are now forced to do exactly this, leaving an estimated 6-to-7 million young children without any pre-school or after-school care, and millions more in informal and often substandard child care arrangements. Equally important, for teenagers as well as adult women, are a full range of reproductive health services, from contraception to abortion to prenatal care. In the past three years, access to these services has been steadily reduced. But for women, these services mean the "right to control our own bodies" and are a precondition for economic security.

In the face of the right's assault, we need to renew the longstanding feminist commitment to government-funded social services. For the short term, the first priority is to reverse the cutbacks in government spending for low-income housing, day care centers, refuges (which have depended heavily on federal grants), and other services. In the long term, we need to build up these services, not as stop-gap measures, but as a vital part of our social infrastructure that meets the critical needs of a vast sector of the population. Services that have heretofore been limited by narrowly defined eligibility criteria (such as subsidized day care) should be expanded, because they are necessary and because expansion will ensure a broad constituency of support and public involvement. Finally, services that have been offered as "commodities" to more or less passive "consumers" (as is true of most medical care) should be redesigned to increase client participation and influence. There is a wealth of experience to draw on: health centers and refuges run by women and child care centers run by community groups are only some of the examples of services organized to involve and empower clients. The democratic spirit that infuses such "alternative" service institutions, combined with government responsibility for sustained, adequate, and national funding, demonstrates an important direction for the reform of the American welfare state.

THE MEANING OF THE "GENDER GAP"

Political expediency is clearly a factor in the assault on the social welfare programs. The Reagan administration does not depend on the poor for votes, and their lack of organizational resources makes effective resistance at the national level difficult. Furthermore, the fragmentation of the American social welfare programs has taken its toll in fragmentation and division among beneficiaries. But this overlooks a politically critical fact: the American poor are disproportionately women. With the revival of feminism in the late 1960s, women have developed a considerable organizational capacity and a consciousness of common interests that cut across class lines. As a result, the Reagan administration's policies are galvanizing a broad movement that joins together middle-class, working-class, and poor women.

The women's movement of the last two decades, like that of the late nineteenth century, has looked to government as the guarantor of women's rights, as in the intense mobilization for the Equal Rights Amendment (ERA), and as a guarantor of economic security. As early as 1967, the "bill of rights" adopted at the first national conference of NOW called for government action to alleviate poverty, to enforce laws against sex discrimination in employment, and to improve the circumstances of older women through changes in the Social Security system. Ten years later, when thousands of women gathered for the First National Women's Conference at Houston, they passed a far-ranging series of resolutions calling, among other things, for a major federal role in the provision of child care services, a federal program of national health insurance, a federal policy of full employment, and increases in federal funding for AFDC and other income-support programs to "provide an adequate standard of living." Taken as a whole, the Houston resolutions amount to a demand not only for greater federal intervention against sex discrimination, but for the creation of an adequate social welfare system for all Americans.

In the years that have passed since the Houston conference, the need for expanded and reliable social welfare programs has become even more acute. For one thing, the experience of the seventies shows that employment, by itself, is not a solution to women's poverty: in what are typically "women's jobs," full-time and year-round work does not necessarily take one above the poverty level. Despite the ups and downs of the business cycle, the expansion of low-paid "women's work" continues, and points to the continued need for public income supports and services for women, whether they are employed or not. Furthermore, a growing proportion of poor women are mothers of young children. Even with a vast expansion of child care services, some women may prefer to remain at home with their small children rather than do double duty as full-time employees and full-time homemakers. Poor women, and especially single mothers, should have this option just as the wives of the affluent do, and social welfare programs should make the choice possible.

These are the reasons, then, that women, particularly feminists, now can lead the way in resisting the attempt to destroy the welfare state. The Reagan administration still waves the banner of laissez faire, but this banner is tattered and unconvincing. The public economy exists, in reality and in the understanding of most Americans. The central political question that has emerged is not whether government will play a large role in American life, but who will pay, and who will gain from what government does. The significance of the steady stream of poll data showing the strong disapproval by women of the Reagan policies is that women have been the first to recognize the question, and to offer the answer of resounding support for government policies to promote economic security and equality.

IV. CREATING REAL NATIONAL SECURITY

GORDON ADAMS

THE American defense budget has doubled since 1980 and will triple by 1988, according to administration proposals. In 1984 Americans will spend $3,200 per household on national defense; between 1984 and 1988, each household will spend $20,000. Military spending now takes fifty cents of every income-tax dollar, a bill which by 1988 will rise to over sixty cents per dollar. By 1986, Americans will be spending more on defense than at any period, whether of peace or war, since 1945.

The defense budget is out of control, unaccountable to taxpayers and elected representatives alike. Criticism of this trend keeps growing at home, as does international uncertainty about the role the United States is playing in the world:

- The call for a nuclear weapons freeze, once a fringe movement, has the support of 75 percent of the American people, has been approved by popular referenda in nine states and many cities, and has been endorsed by the United States House of Representatives.
- An administration deeply skeptical of arms control was forced by public opinion to open arms control talks with the Soviet

Union in Geneva, although there is some doubt as to the sincerity and feasibility of its proposals.

- Europeans are severely divided over the wisdom of deploying new nuclear weapons on their soil.
- The growing crisis in Central America, persistent problems in the Middle East, and upheavals in the rest of the developing world make many Americans suspect that government policy is bringing us closer to war.
- Repeated investigations of defense spending have exposed waste and inefficiency, from the M-1 tank, which drives poorly, to the Bradley amphibious infantry fighting vehicle, which can't float, to aircraft parts, which cost many times more than they should.
- Both conservative and liberal voices have warned that weapons costs and the defense budget itself are out of control. This will mean later expenditures much larger than expected, with fearsome consequences for the economy.
- Broad segments of the American population, many of whom never before worried about military spending, are concerned about the impact that the defense budget will have on federal budget deficits, interest rates, capital supplies, future industrial investment, and the creation of new jobs in a still depressed economy.

Something is desperately wrong with present American national security policy. For the first time in over thirty-five years, ordinary Americans are engaged in a debate about matters once left to the experts. As the risk of conflict grows, increasingly large segments of the American population search for an alternative.

CURRENT CHOICES

The Reagan program is clear: The United States must not only be prepared to deter the Soviet Union with its nuclear forces; it must also be able to "prevail" in a nuclear conflict over a "protracted" period of time. This goal requires massive additions to the American arsenal—the MX missile, the Trident submarine and missile, the B-1 bomber, 7,000 cruise missiles (on land, at sea, and in the air), a future stealth bomber, ballistic missile defense, *Star Wars* space weapons, and civil defense.

Although the nuclear program is growing—by over 30 percent in real dollars in fiscal year 1984—conventional military spending remains more than 75 percent of the nation's military budget. New programs include anti-armor missiles, tanks, armored personnel carriers, helicopters, fighters, battleship reactivation, aircraft carriers, and a proposed 600-ship navy. All the services are receiving new conventional weapons at a rapid rate.

One alternative policy emerges from a congressional group called the military reform caucus. Members include Senator Gary Hart (D-CO), moderate Representative James Courter (R-NJ), and conservative Representative William Whitehurst (R-VA). This group appeals to a common denominator: a search for systems that perform well and can be easily operated and maintained. But this search for efficiency poses no fundamental political criticism of the Reagan administration's defense policies and provides no framework for making *choices* about defense policy in response to national security needs. The military reform carcus espouses no views about the nature of the Soviet threat, the military balance in Europe, or the government's claimed need for rapid intervention in the Third World. As a result, those who support much higher levels of defense spending can rally to its banner as easily as others who see reform as a way to lower the defense budget. Until these security issues have been tackled, budget reductions will be, at best, marginal.

Another position current in the Democratic party calls for a halt to the nuclear arms race. Our national security, in this view, can no longer depend on continued expansion of the nuclear deterrent. Strategic nuclear forces need to be stabilized, or frozen, with reductions to follow, in order to avoid a holocaust.

Those who advocate nuclear arms control differ on the need for conventional military spending. In one view, nuclear arms control and reductions would require major increases in conventional military spending. This argument for a "conventional build-up" does not noticeably differ from the administration in its view of the international environment—hostile, dominated by the Soviet threat, and requiring large increases in U.S. military spending. It diverts, but does not slow, the arms race.

In the opposing view, nuclear arms control need not be accompanied by a conventional build-up, because the "conventional force balance" between NATO and the Warsaw Pact is not nearly as unfavorable as it is often portrayed. This last choice—reductions in nuclear forces without increase in conventional arms—entails serious efforts toward arms control in general: negotiations in Geneva on European nuclear forces and strategic arms; a U.S. declaration of "no first use" of nuclear weapons; measures to reduce the likelihood of accidental nuclear war; and above all, negotiations toward a bilateral, verifiable nuclear weapons freeze between the United States and the Soviet Union.

Desirable as these goals may be, the arms control/freeze position does not by itself provide a viable alternative. Its supporters have not set out the details of the national security framework within which a freeze would be possible, or addressed the details of defense budgets and spending, conventional forces, and U.S. policies toward the Southern Tier. Most arms control/freeze advocates do not deal directly with international reality. Too often, they assume that "human interaction" between Russians and Americans will be enough to stop the arms race. Human interaction is important; but it is not sufficient in a real and dangerous world of nations that have conflicting definitions of their interests. A straight line toward disarmament is not realistic, and lacks appeal to the vast majority of Americans simply because it fails to deal with the full agenda of national security issues.

An alternative program for American national security should start from clear, common principles which many Americans can share. These principles should lead to a redefinition of national security aims, which, in turn, should determine the missions, equipment, and size of the armed forces we require for national defense. The defense budget, in the end, should reflect the costs of a commonsense national security policy.

Every administration would argue that it has prepared defense budgets in just this way. In reality, the preparation of the defense budget frequently happens in reverse.[1] Budget planners tend to start with what they have and with last year's budget numbers—and add on the next year. The national security planning system responds not only to real-world issues, but frequently to bureaucratic pressures and to defense industry manufacturers seeking to remain in the weapons business. These pressures are multiplied by members of Congress who make defense budget decisions or represent districts closely tied to defense industries. This process, sometimes called the "iron triangle," rarely starts with basic principles.

THE COMMONSENSE ALTERNATIVE

The alternative proposal expounded in this essay works from the following five basic ideas, which contrast sharply with the administration's policies:

- The United States and the Soviet Union are condemned to live with each other, regardless of each country's view of the other. Anything else would be suicide for both countries. Both have a national interest in toning down the arms competition, stabilizing the nuclear arms race, reducing strategic weapons, and moving military resources to productive investment. This means ending several new strategic weapons programs and engaging in bilateral talks for arms control.
- The European military balance has been stable for three decades, and NATO maintains a more than adequate capability—nuclear and conventional—to deter a European war. Despite asymmetries in forces, the two pacts are in stalemate. More important, neither NATO nor the Warsaw Pact wants a military conflict in Western Europe, and, despite the fact that each side spends billions with such a contingency in mind, neither pact actually *expects* such a war.
- Warfare and civil conflict have been endemic in the Southern Tier of the globe since the end of the Second World War. Over one hundred new nations have emerged from the shadow of

colonialism, and they must deal with some of the most serious problems in human history. These problems, and not meddling by the Soviet Union or imperial expansion by the United States, are at the heart of the Southern Tier dilemma. Neither the United States nor the Soviet Union helps address these problems by expanding ocean-going navies, increasing rapid deployment forces, or supporting crash programs of foreign arms sales. The national security alternative for the Southern Tier must focus attention on the area's real problems, while maintaining an adequate military capability to secure essential interests: protection of citizens, security of sea lanes, and international peacekeeping missions.

· There must be major changes in the way weapons are purchased. Weapons cost far more than planned, and there is no incentive for cost control in the Defense Department or in the defense industry. Reform is needed to eliminate wasteful spending and to ensure that weapons choices are linked to national security goals and not to the survival of bureaucrats or corporations.

· National security requires a healthy economy. The rapid growth of defense spending makes it more difficult to solve our economic problems. The defense budget increases federal borrowing, drains capital markets, helps keep interest rates high, and contributes to deficits. It also diverts productivity-enhancing research investment and weakens our ability to create new employment.

THE UNITED STATES AND THE SOVIET UNION: IS THERE A WAY?

Our relationship with the Soviet Union is shrouded in myths and obscured further by the Reagan administration's exaggerated rhetoric. This administration is not the first to exaggerate Soviet military capabilities as a way of greasing the skids for the defense budget in Congress. Still, it is true that the military power of the Soviet Union has grown; it would be naive to assume otherwise. On the other hand, it is equally naive to assume that American military superiority is or could be great enough to frighten the Soviet Union into some kind of submission.

Fundamentally, American national security policy is impossible to define simply in terms of the Soviet "threat." This is a slender and frayed justification for defense budgets. National security cannot start from a vision which sees all world events as the product of tensions between the United States and the Soviet Union. It must start, first, from positive goals; however, it is crucial to put aside a few prevailing myths.

MYTH: *"From 1970 to 1981, the Soviets out-invested the U.S. in defense by about half a trillion dollars in constant 1984 dollars."*[2]

Soviet defense spending, in dollars or in rubles, is not known, even to the Defense Department. Official figures show a Soviet defense budget of only 17 billion rubles (the artificial conversion rate is $1.37 to the ruble). The ruble is not convertible to the dollar outside the Soviet Union, so there is no way to know how much Soviet defense spending actually represents *in dollars.*

To circumvent the inadequate information, the United States Central Intelligence Agency (CIA) estimates Soviet defense spending by counting Soviet troops and Soviet military equipment and estimating what it would cost the United States to reproduce the same troops and equipment. In other words, we apply our military wages (dramatically higher than Soviet wages) and our prices for producing high-technology military equipment (also higher than Soviet prices) to the Soviet forces.[3] The result is to overestimate what the Soviet Union actually spends. Every time U.S. military wages increase, the CIA estimate of Soviet military wages also rises. Every time the defense industry here experiences inflation or encounters cost overruns on equipment, the CIA estimate of the cost of Soviet weapons rises as well. The intelligence establishment recognizes the weakness of this methodology. In the spring of 1983, CIA and Defense Intelligence Agency analysts reported that they had overestimated the real dollar growth rate of Soviet military spending by *at least one-third* over the past eight years![4]

Another weakness of such spending comparisons is that they generally avoid comparing the two alliances and focus, instead, on the two superpowers. Even given the inadequacies of the methodology, a comparison of the defense spending of the United States *and its NATO allies* over a ten-year period with the spending by the Soviet Union and *its Warsaw Pact allies* over the same decade shows that NATO outspent the Warsaw Pact by $250 billion.[5] Another comparison, using figures from the International Institute for Strategic Studies, concludes that "the United States and its NATO allies outspent the Soviet Union and its Warsaw Pact allies on defense by more than $300 billion in the past decade."[6] The "defense spending gap" is a myth.

M Y T H : *"While our principal adversaries engaged in the greatest build-up of military power seen in modern times, our own invest-ment in forces and weapons continued to decline until very recently."*[7]

Did the United States let its defense spending decline? Did the United States allow its strategic forces to deteriorate during the 1970s while the Soviet Union improved its deterrent? Chart 1 traces U.S. defense spending since 1940 in constant (uninflated) dollars. Over the long term, as the graph shows, U.S. defense spending did decline in real dollars each time the United States ended its involvement in a war (World War II, Korea, Vietnam). This decline tells nothing, however, about U.S. military strength; it tells us that a war has ended and the troops are home.

The relatively constant level of peacetime defense spending from Korea to Vietnam and from Vietnam to the Reagan era suggests that our defense commitment has been fairly constant. Even when defense budgets fell in the 1970s, they remained consistent with past peacetime eras in real dollars. The sharp upward turn during the Reagan administration does not show recovery; it shows that this administration is engaging in the most rapid *increase* in peacetime military spending in American history. By 1985, Reagan military spending will surpass previous *wartime* levels since 1945.

The administration argues that U.S. strategic forces are old and points to the Titan missile and the B-52 bomber (both over

PEACETIME MILITARY BUILD-UP
The Historical Context

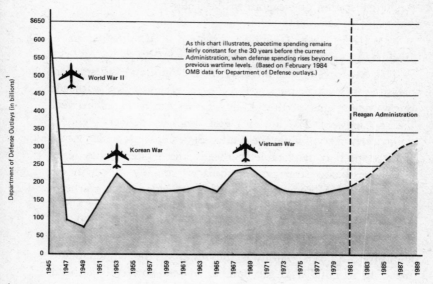

As this chart illustrates, peacetime spending remains fairly constant for the 30 years before the current Administration, when defense spending rises beyond previous wartime levels. (Based on February 1984 OMB data for Department of Defense outlays.)

Department of Defense Outlays (in billions)[1]

World War II

Korean War

Vietnam War

Reagan Administration

[1] In constant 1985 dollars

From Defense Budget Project.

twenty years old) as examples. These selective examples exaggerate the point. It is, indeed, true that official U.S. spending on strategic forces was lower in the 1970s than in the 1960s. Yet from 1970 through the last budget of the Carter administration (fiscal year 1981), the Defense Department spent $100 billion on U.S. strategic forces, systematically modernizing them: completing deployment of 550 Minuteman III missiles, each fitted with three warheads and more accurate guidance; research and development on the MX missile; new electronics, engines, and wings for the B-52, at a cost equal to the original cost of building the B-52 fleet; redesigning B-52's to carry cruise missiles; development and production of the air-launched, sea-launched, and ground-launched cruise missiles; development and production of the Trident submarine and its C-4 missile; and research and development on the Trident D-5 missile.

The logic of the nuclear arms race seems inexorable—the United States invested heavily in the 1960s; the Soviet Union expanded its forces in the 1970s; the United States has begun a new generation of weapons in the 1980s.

MYTH : *The Soviet Union has achieved a "definite margin of superiority" over the United States.*[8]

This assertion is meaningless. "Bean counting" the standard measures of strategic nuclear forces—delivery vehicles, warheads, throw-weight, and accuracy—shows that parity exists between the superpowers. The Soviet Union leads in delivery vehicles, with nearly 2,500, while the United States has just under 2,000. With respect to deliverable warheads, the United States leads, with over 9,000 strategic warheads to roughly 7,000 in the Soviet arsenal. Moreover, the United States added 5,200 warheads to its strategic arsenal during the 1970s, while the Soviet Union added 4,200, thereby increasing the American lead. In throw-weight, the Soviet Union has an edge, with larger and more explosive warheads. This was the result of the United States' planning to build a larger number of less powerful warheads which could reach their targets more accurately.

With respect to conventional forces, analyses that suggest an imbalance usually compare only U.S. and Soviet forces. Such force comparisons are a tricky business. Simple "bean counting" will not do; one has to look, as well, at a country's strategy, history of warfare, military readiness, foreign policy objectives, and, especially, its geographic situation.

The Soviet Union clearly has a larger tank force, armor capability, coastal navy, and air defense system than the United States. This is to be expected, given its history of repeated invasion by other nations, the Soviet occupation of potentially hostile countries on its western frontier, its long borders with unfriendly nations, little naval experience, and potential exposure to a two-front war in Europe and Asia.

The United States, by contrast, has clear superiority in air transport, long-range bombers, ocean-going naval vessels, sea transport capabilities, longer-range fighter-bombers, and antitank weapons. This, too, is predictable, given the few invasions of United States territory, the country's history as an ocean-going power, its military involvement overseas, and focus on advanced-technology weapons. United States and Soviet forces are asymmetrical, but not because one power has engaged in a historically unprecedented arms development while the other (the United States) stood with one hand tied behind its back. Neither force is automatically superior to the other.

General John W. Vessey, Jr., Chairman of the Joint Chiefs of Staff, testified on May 11, 1982, that he preferred U.S. forces: "But overall, would I trade with Marshal Ogarkov? Not on your life."[9]

MYTH: *U.S. strategic forces face a "window of vulnerability."*[10]

The "window of vulnerability" is used to justify almost any assertion about the military balance. Its real meaning, however, has always been quite specific: the alleged vulnerability of the 1,052 U.S. land-based strategic missiles to a totally successful Soviet first strike. This worst-case analysis, carried out by the Air Force in the 1970s, suggested that under certain conditions, as much as 90 percent of the U.S. land-based missile force might be destroyed. This analysis stimulated demands in the Air Force for a mobile, land-based missile—the MX.

This worst-case analysis is highly suspect. It is unlikely that the Soviet Union would have the advantage of such a surprise attack, given United States monitoring from outer space. Moreover, since ballistic missiles are never tested across the poles, it is unlikely that all Soviet missiles would behave as projected.

More telling, it is unlikely that the American response to such a first strike would be to sit idly by and let the Soviet Union exercise its will. A massive response is likely, and the capability for such a response remains ample. Only 23.2 percent of U.S. strategic warheads are on these land-based missiles; another 25 percent are on manned bombers; and over 50 percent on invulnerable submarines. Even in the worst case, 75 percent of U.S. strategic forces would be left unaffected.

By contrast, 70 percent of Soviet warheads are on land-based missiles. If anything, the Soviet Union has a "window of vulnerability" in relation to the more accurate U.S. forces.

MYTH: *In a "protracted" nuclear war, the United States should plan to "prevail," or: it is possible to imagine fighting, controlling, winning, and surviving a nuclear war.*

The Reagan administration has argued that the United States needs to have nuclear forces capable not only of preventing a Soviet first strike, but of responding to such an attack, sustaining that response over an extended period of time, and, in the end, "prevailing." As a result, the administration program for the next generation of nuclear forces calls for a survivable war-fighting potential.

The often-quoted comments of T. K. Jones, now working on strategic policy in the Office of the Secretary of Defense, illustrates how ludicrous this program is. Jones asserted that nuclear war will be survivable if only there are "enough shovels" to go around.[11] In 1982, Arms Control and Disarmament Agency adviser Colin Gray commented on nuclear strategy as follows:

> We have to target, as discreetly as we can, the Soviet state as opposed to the Russian people. Now we can only do that to a limited degree—the state is to a large degree co-located with the Russian people, unfortunately. But we think we're talking into the Russian value structure.[12]

Behind such comedy, however, lies a serious purpose: maintaining or restoring superiority in strategic nuclear power and developing the capability of fighting a nuclear war. A considerable number of strategic analysts, however, including former Defense Secretary Robert McNamara, former National Security Advisor McGeorge Bundy, and a number of retired NATO and U.S. military officers, argue that a nuclear war, once started, would quickly become uncontrollable.

An alternative national security policy must move us away from these myths. *Stability* is the watchword of such an alternative. Americans and Soviets need not like each other; neither country has to show full trust for the other. Both sides need only agree that the next step in the arms race could result in mutual suicide.

The technology necessary to implement and verify arms control agreements such as the SALT II treaty (still not ratified by the United States), a mutual total ban on nuclear tests, and even a bilateral nuclear weapons freeze does exist.[13] Such agreements would not freeze us at a level of inferiority.[14] Rather, they would accomplish a significant purpose: closing the door on the next stage of the arms race.

This first step should soon be followed by mutual reductions in nuclear arsenals. Lower numbers of nuclear weapons would actually enhance security; higher levels lead only to greater insecurity. "Nuclear superiority" is a phrase without meaning so long as each superpower retains, as it does, a deterrent that could survive a first strike. It is easy, and relatively inexpensive, to deny superiority to the other; it is practically impossible and prohibitively expensive to achieve it oneself.

CONFLICT IN EUROPE: IS IT LIKELY?

In the name of national security, the United States spends half of its military budget on the contingency of a European war. Over 250,000 U.S. troops are stationed in Europe, along with considerable armor, munitions, fighters, and over 6,000 nuclear warheads. Both NATO and the Warsaw Pact are armed to the teeth, as if military conflicts were due to break out at any moment.

Even some critics of aspects of the Reagan military program suggest that conventional force planning for Western Europe is crucial. Yet national security policy with respect to Western Europe has a yawning credibility gap. There is no evidence that *either alliance*, NATO or the Warsaw Pact, actually expects a war. Neither alliance plans to carry out such a conflict today, and both acknowledge that it would be a disaster.

The European military balance, moreover, is not nearly as negative for NATO as the Reagan administration implies. As former Secretary of Defense Robert McNamara described it, the European theater is subject to considerable "threat inflation":

> Soviet conventional strength is not as great as many state it to be, and the NATO conventional weakness is not as great as it is frequently said to be. Therefore, the conventional balance is not as favorable to the Soviets as is often assumed.
>
> . . . [W]e overstate the Soviets' force and we understate ours, and we therefore greatly overstate the imbalance. This is not something that is new; it has been going on for years.[15]

Conventional "bean counting" in Europe actually favors NATO, which has slightly more personnel under arms in Central Europe (2.8 million versus 2.6 million), and counters the Soviet tank advantage (27,000 versus 12,000) with antitank weapons (190,000 versus 70,000). NATO surface combatant ships outnumber the Warsaw Pact by two to one, and NATO retains naval aircraft and long-range fighter-bomber superiority.[16]

Bean counting, strategic history, and geography alike suggest that "Soviet superiority" in Europe is a myth. William Kaufmann of the Brookings Institution suggests that NATO's only serious weakness is in its ability to resupply troops once a war is under way; this can be remedied. The scenario of a sudden Soviet rush to the sea he considers virtually impossible.[17]

An alternative national security policy for Europe should start from these realities. The real question in Europe is not how to restore superiority, but how to reduce the risk that the war nobody wants or expects will happen anyway.

Nuclear weapons in Europe are the first problem to solve. The Soviet Union has been building and deploying the new SS-20 intermediate-range missile while it slowly retires the older, less mobile SS-4 and SS-5's. There is little doubt, however, that total NATO nuclear capabilities, short- and medium-range alike, outweigh those of the Soviet Union—6,000 versus under 3,000 warheads. No new nuclear weapons are needed on either side, and the goal of stability would be served by immediate reductions on the part of *both sides*, not by the deployment of the Pershing II and ground-launched cruise missiles planned by our government. A commonsense alternative would include a declaration of "no first use" of nuclear weapons by the United States (the Soviet Union has already done so); serious bilateral talks in Geneva for an agreement on mutual reduction of nuclear forces; and the gradual withdrawal from Europe, over time, of nuclear weapons not usable in the European theater.

This change does not require massive increases in conventional arms spending. An alternative policy should strike a balance between force improvements, training, readiness, spending, and supplies on the one hand, and negotiations within Europe and with the Soviet Union on the other, to reduce forces in a balanced and mutual way. Talks on such force reductions have been under way for several years in Vienna, but making progress in them a priority would be a dramatically new step.

THE SOUTHERN TIER: WHAT DOES SECURITY MEAN?

The sudden emergence of over one hundred independent new nations, carved out of European colonial empires, is the most dramatic geopolitical change of the twentieth century. American political memory is short; we tend to forget that, for these nations, economic development was tied to colonial investment. This has left many Southern Tier countries vulnerable to sudden shifts in global trade, investment, and currency values. Postcolonial investments and population shifts have meant extreme social rifts, continued poverty, and disease for many.

Change and upheaval are likely to continue in the Southern Tier for many years. Economic development will be uneven; social stresses will sometimes erupt into violence; democratic politics will rarely be chosen; disputes over frontiers are likely. Change is inevitable, and American policy needs to understand it.

The Reagan administration is committed to a major increase in U.S. capabilities for military response to Southern Tier developments. The navy has plans to increase the fleet to 600 ships, including two new nuclear aircraft carrier battle groups beyond the 13 already available. The military approach to the

Southern Tier also includes a major restructuring of U.S. intervention forces by emphasizing the importance of the Rapid Development Force (RDF). Originally, the RDF proposal was a modest one, for roughly 110,000 troops. Under Reagan, it has grown to over 225,000, including a large headquarters staff in Tampa, Florida, new cargo aircraft (50–100), new sealift, and pre-positioning of equipment overseas. The additional spending for such a force has been estimated minimally at $4 billion per year; it could be as high as $15 billion per year.

An alternative Southern Tier policy must take a more commonsense approach. Public reaction to events in Central America suggests that many Americans understand this. Massive overseas intervention and rapid deployment are not welcome. The Vietnam trauma, sometimes described as an unacceptable "syndrome," contained a valuable lesson: the United States cannot determine the changes taking place in Third World countries, nor prevent them by military means. National security would be enhanced, instead, by learning to work with at least some of these changes. American influence in the Southern Tier depends, centrally, on diplomatic and economic strategies that assist economic growth. Only through development will the stresses and strains of the Southern Tier be eased, a process that may take decades. In addition, the United States would do well to acknowledge political changes that have already taken place, whatever our judgment of the results—for example in Cuba, Angola, and Vietnam.

A military component has a place in this alternative. Although it is argued that 600 ships are necessary in order to keep up with the Soviet naval threat, the number 600 has no magic; it was chosen arbitrarily. The United States already has overwhelming superiority as an ocean-going naval power. The Rapid Deployment Force is also unnecessary. For many years, the United States has had the world's most powerful mobility force, combining airborne and amphibious troops, especially the 180,000-strong Marine Corps. The United States also far surpasses any other nation in its airlift capability.

BANGS AND BUCKS: ARE WE GETTING THE BEST SECURITY FOR OUR MONEY?

Within the first six months of 1983, no fewer than eight separate sources, several from the top level of the Defense Department, suggested that defense spending was out of control. The future defense plans of the Reagan administration could be significantly underfunded, creating severe budget problems; the contracting process was ineffective in holding down weapons' costs, and taxpayer funds were being wasted in defense procurement.[18]

This spending spree has opened the door to serious readiness problems. The fastest growing part of the defense budget has been under the heading of "defense investment"—researching and purchasing weapons, and military construction. The share of the defense budget going to the accounts most directly related to military readiness—personnel, and operations and maintenance (O&M)—is declining. Although measures of the weapons and readiness spending are rough, the changing proportions suggest serious budget problems in the future. As more weapons are added, more personnel and operations and maintenance money will be required to keep them ready. Since those accounts are not keeping pace, there is growing concern that a rapid build-up will actually decrease the readiness of the U.S. military forces.

Eliminating some new weapons programs would help solve another major problem in national security policy. The Defense Department is encountering criticism that many new weapons will not be able to fulfill their missions. The "military reform group" in Congress notes that the M-1 tank has engine and drive train problems; the M-2 armored personnel carrier has too little room for soldiers and is a large sitting target for attack; the F-18 fighter, because it was designed also to be a bomber, has had its range reduced; the Copperhead missile is much less accurate than the contractor promised; the AH-64 helicopter was designed to help ground troops, but could be a suicide vehicle for its crew.

WEAPONS V. READINESS
WHERE IS THE DEFENSE DOLLAR REALLY GOING?

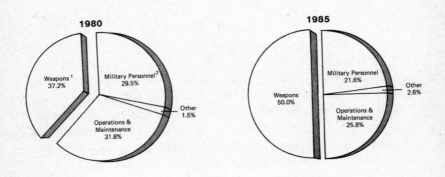

1980

Weapons [1]
37.2%

Military Personnel [2]
29.5%

Other
1.5%

Operations &
Maintenance
31.8%

1985

Military Personnel
21.6%

Other
2.6%

Weapons
50.0%

Operations &
Maintenance
25.8%

Note:

[1] Weapons includes research and development, procurement, military construction and nuclear warhead programs in the Department of Energy.

[2] Military Personnel includes personnel and retirement pay.

Source:
Based on data from **Budget of the United States Government FY 1985**, OMB, February 1, 1984

Totals may not add up to 100% due to rounding.

From Defense Budget Project.

    The Defense Department has defended its weapons and the way it buys them. In April of 1981, Deputy Secretary of Defense Frank Carlucci announced thirty-two reforms in the buying practices of the Defense Department, promising lower costs. These reforms, however, were poorly designed. Instead of restricting the defense budget to ensure spending discipline, they took the lid off the budget, making greater amounts of funding available to planners at the start of a weapons program.

    The procurement reforms of the Reagan administration have had equally little effect on controlling costs. Only two of the reforms even dealt with costs. One called for taking a contractor's past performance into account in awarding future contracts. It was found largely unenforceable and dropped, while Lockheed and Rockwell, both of which have had cost problems in the past, received new production contracts for aircraft. The other reform called for increased competition in defense contracting and remains a focus of concern at the Defense Department. However, the July 1983 Grace Commission report on Defense Department management noted that more than 90 percent of Defense Department contracts continued to be awarded without competitive bidding—which suggests that this reform is not being implemented.[19]

An alternative national security policy must include major changes in the way weapons and budgets are planned and purchased. If readiness is needed for our military forces, then readiness, not weapons buying, should be the focus of a budget. But "readiness for what?" is a crucial question that military reformers too often fail to answer. National security requirements should guide that answer: a stable, lower level of deterrence; a ready, capable, though smaller presence in Western Europe; ocean-going and mobility forces adequate to protect the United States and its citizens, keep sea lanes open, and provide for international peacekeeping. With dramatically lower purchases of unnecessary new equipment, such readiness should be much easier to sustain.

The buying process also needs to be changed. The Defense Department depends almost entirely on its contractors for the cost data it uses in evaluating a proposal for a new weapon or in raising a contract price. There is far too little independent Pentagon estimation of costs. A truly independent cost analysis group in the Pentagon could help with this problem. Greater competition would also reduce contract costs. The Defense Science Board has estimated that enhanced competition could save as much as 15–20 percent in an average contract.

Despite the growing criticism of Defense Department procurement practices, little has changed in this administration. A House Armed Services Committee Staff Briefing on Operations and Maintenance suggests why procurement reform is difficult:

O&M [operations and maintenance] is handicapped when competing against highly organized Washington lobbies actively seeking more dollars for various procurement and R&D [research and development] programs. . . . [A] Washington representative for a procurement program would have little problem conveying to you the effect [of a cut] on his program. . . . This constituency for procurement and R&D works independently of the services, while the troops in the field are almost wholly reliant upon service sponsors.[20]

The simple truth about the Defense Department is that its work is only partly intended to serve national security. The defense market is one of the largest in the American economy—over $100 billion in defense contracts is awarded each year. It is a concentrated market—the leading twenty-five contractors regularly receive roughly 50 percent of all prime defense contracts, in dollar value. And it is a steady business.

Defense contractors who want to maintain their defense business have powerful allies. Members of Congress survive through reelection and must, therefore, respond to the needs of their districts. Congressional members who come from districts containing defense plants or who sit on the Armed Services or Defense Appropriations Committees tend to support higher defense spending and contracts for firms in their districts.

Contractors maintain Washington offices to monitor congressional and Defense Department developments and to seek access to and influence over decisions. Audits by the Defense Contract Audit Agency of the Washington offices of five leading contractors—Boeing, General Dynamics, Grumman, Lockheed, and Rockwell International—show that in the mid-1970s, each company was spending an average of $1.5 million a year on its Washington effort. The bulk of this expenditure was being billed to the companies' defense contracts. Defense contractors also make considerable use of a more recent governmental relations tool—the Political Action Committee (PAC)—to make contributions to key politicians. The eight major contractors, for example, spent over $2 million through their PAC's in the late 1970s, most of it in contributions to key members of Congress. Contractors also find other techniques helpful in maintaining their political influence, such as hiring retired Pentagon employees and mobilizing local communities to lobby for contracts.

Together, defense contractors, key members of Congress, and Pentagon bureaucrats make up an "Iron Triangle"—a network of policymakers who are linked through information, access, influence, and, above all, money.[21] Real change in national security policy may only be possible when the structure of relationships among them has changed. Even here, some limited steps would help. Legislation should be passed that makes it illegal for former Defense Department people to go to work for defense contractors with whom they have dealt. One could require greater disclosure of information on subcontracting in order to track the emergence of political constituencies for new weapons, and limit Political Action Committee campaign contributions. At the root of this triangle lies the heavy dependency of some firms on defense business. Real changes may require a reexamination of the structure of ownership in defense. Defense manufacturing is already inefficient; one can hardly argue that public ownership of these facilities would be more inefficient. At the very least, a more direct public role in the contracting process would increase the accountability of the Iron Triangle to elected public officials and the taxpayer.

CAN THE ECONOMY SURVIVE THE MILITARY BUILD-UP?

Our national security is closely tied to the state of the American economy. The importance of today's military spending may lie in the degree to which rapidly expanding military spending is making it more difficult to solve our economic problems. Today, budget deficits are out of control, American productivity has declined, and new jobs are hard to find while millions of Americans remain unemployed.

Common sense suggests that defense spending, the only federal spending program growing in real dollars, has something to do with the growing budget deficit, which the Congressional Budget Office says will accumulate to a level of $1.3 trillion between 1983 and 1988. Defense spending takes up over 40 percent of general tax revenues; combined with military programs in the Energy Department, NASA, and the Veteran's Administration, defense's share rises up to over 50 percent. Controlling budget deficits in the future will depend, in part, on controlling defense spending.

The federal government spends seventy cents of every research and development dollar on defense-related research. This leaves only thirty cents for research that might contribute directly to productivity growth and job creation. The Defense Department argues that its research investments are good for the economy, yet defense technology has now become so sophisticated and expensive that its commercial applications are few.

Even jobs may be affected negatively by rapid growth in defense spending. The defense budget is often sold as a jobs program, healthy for local economy, and workers in many American communities do depend on the defense dollar for their jobs. Well over 2 million Americans work on defense contracts. Within the defense industry, however, new jobs are not emerging. Although the McDonnell-Douglas corporation does four times the amount of defense contracting today that it did in 1970, its labor force has shrunk from 92,000 to 72,000 over the same period.[22] This same change is taking place with other defense contractors. The defense business is becoming more "capital intensive"—more and more of the defense dollar is going into raw materials, research, technology, and new machinery, and less and less into new jobs. Moreover, the defense industry does not hire much from groups suffering from the highest unemployment rates in America: minorities, women, less-skilled and less-educated people. Almost any other form of federal spending creates more jobs for these workers.

The security policy proposed here would generate resource savings from the defense budget and minimize economic damage. It needs, as well, to include a defense conversion program with plans for specific defense facilities; joint planning between localities and the federal government; aid to communities that depend on the defense dollar; legislation for pension and health benefit portability, retraining, and relocation assistance for defense industry workers; and targeting of federal spending to diversify and convert defense plants.

The Reagan administration's military build-up has not only failed to provide greater security, it has left Americans more fearful of war, damaged the American economy, led to runaway and wasteful defense spending, short-changed vast sectors of American society in desperate need, and weakened what control Congress and the public have over the federal budget. National security has declined as military spending has grown.

It is vital to define a more coherent, sensible, and progressive national security policy, which would appeal, moreover, to a broad spectrum of Americans. Our relationship with the rest of the world, which now seems to promise war, would change dramatically: it would enable peaceful and realistic relations with the Soviet Union, it would reduce the risks of war in Europe, and it would bring about a reappraisal of Third World develop-ment anchored not in the pursuit of arms but in economic growth and necessary social change.

The damage done by uncontrolled military spending within our country could also begin to be undone. Reagan's budget priorities are not only manifestly unfair to whole segments of American society, but runaway defense allocations promise to squeeze the domestic sector even further. Moreover, as weapons spending surges ahead, the appetite of Pentagon budget planners will grow, further distorting the budget. Small businesses that need capital, unions whose members need jobs, and low-income Americans out of work will see solutions to their problems recede into the distance. Americans who have awakened to the security dilemma will realize that the Pentagon is totally closed off and the Congress virtually unreachable. Those who struggle for a bilateral nuclear weapons freeze while ninety-seven of their supporters in the House of Representatives vote for new strategic weapons have begun to see the risks.

The bill for the Reagan build-up is slowly coming due. The affected constituencies are growing, as is the nationwide debate over national security. Perhaps the most important result of this debate is the first signs that the Iron Triangle, so responsible for defense policy-making for years, is beginning to *weaken and show fissures*. A coherent progressive security policy can be forced through those openings and into the political arena.

NOTES

1. Gordon Adams, "The Political Consequences of the Nuclear Arms Race," in a forthcoming book edited by The Center on Ethics and Public Policy, University of California, and Gordon Adams, "Disarming the Military Subgovernment," *Harvard Journal on Legislation* 14, no. 3 (April 1977): 459–503.

2. White House, Office of Policy Information, *Fairness II: An Executive Briefing Book*, May 1, 1983, Tab. V.

3. Franklyn Holzman, "Are the Soviets Really Outspending the U.S. on Defense?" *International Security* 4, no. 4 (Spring 1980): 86–104; and "Soviet Military Spending: Assessing the Numbers Game," *International Security* 6, no. 4 (Spring 1982): 78–101.

4. Leslie Gelb and Richard Halloran, "CIA Analysts Now Said to Find U.S. Overstated Soviet Arms Rise," *New York Times*, March 3, 1983; Fred Kaplan, "Soviet Arms Budget Debate in U.S.," *Boston Globe*, February 16, 1983.

5. Franklyn Holzman, "Are We Falling Behind the Soviets?" *The Atlantic* (July 1983).

6. Richard Stubbing, "The Imaginary Defense Gap: We Already Outspend Them," *Washington Post*, February 14, 1982.

7. Caspar Weinberger, *Annual Report to the Congress, Fiscal Year 1983* (Washington, D.C.: Government Printing Office, 1983), I–4.

8. President Ronald Reagan, Press Conference, March 31, 1982.

9. Holzman, "Falling Behind?" 14.

10. President Ronald Reagan, Press Conference, October 1, 1981.

11. Robert Scheer, *With Enough Shovels* (New York: Random House, 1982).

12. James Lardner, "The Call of the Hawk's Hawk," *Washington Post*, May 14, 1982.

13. *See* Federation of American Scientists, *Public Interest Report* (September 1982).

14. Randall Forsberg, "A Bilateral Nuclear Weapons Freeze," *Scientific American* (November 1982).

15. Robert Scheer, "Fear of a U.S. First Strike Seen as Cause of Arms Race," *Los Angeles Times*, April 8, 1982.

16. John Collins, *U.S.-Soviet Military Balance: Concepts and Capabilities, 1960–1980* (New York: McGraw-Hill, 1980).

17. William Kaufmann, "The Defense Budget," in *Setting National Priorities*, ed. Joseph A. Pechman (The Brookings Institution, 1983), 63–64.

18. George Kuhn, "Ending Defense Stagnation," in the Heritage Foundation, *Agenda '83* (Washington, D.C.: 1983), 69–114; Gordon Adams, *Controlling Weapons Costs: Can the Pentagon Reforms Work?* (New York: Council on Economic Priorities, 1983); Richard Halloran, "Admiral Says Shoddy Work Adds 50% to Some Arms Cost," *The New York Times*, June 26, 1983; Department of Defense, Office of the Inspector General, *Draft Report on the Audit of the Procurement of Aircraft Engine Spare Parts*, June 21, 1983; and U.S. Air Force, *The Affordable Acquisition Approach Study*, February 9, 1983.
19. *Newsweek*, July 11, 1983; and *Time*, July 11, 1983.
20. Op. cit., p. 5.
21. Gordon Adams, *The Politics of Defense Contracting: The Iron Triangle* (New Brunswick, N.J.: Transaction Press, 1982).
22. As calculated by the Defense Budget Project, Center on Budget and Policy Priorities (Washington, D.C.: 1983).

V. PAYING FOR PROGRESS

ROBERT LEKACHMAN

I N Europe, concern over the costs of social welfare has spread from conservatives to liberals and social democrats, sometimes as a consequence of popular dissatisfaction over the tax burden required to pay for the measures of the welfare state: retirement, unemployment benefits, and medical care. Social welfare consumes a third of the West German Gross National Product and even higher percentages in Sweden and The Netherlands. Many Europeans believe that, at best, future growth rates—negative in the early 1980s—will be smaller than they were in the 1950s and 1960s, when France, West Germany, and Italy celebrated sustained prosperity and rising living standards. On the left, concern over the viability of the welfare state extends beyond financial considerations. Just as nationalizing an enterprise does not automatically turn discontented employees into gratified stockholders, so the sturdiest of safety nets has not increased public happiness, at least as measured by such indices as alcoholism, mental illness, child neglect, and family breakup. Many on the democratic left have begun to question the structures of welfare delivery and to examine the less benign side effects of well-intentioned social protections.

Such responses are not astonishing. The Dutch health system extends practically complete medical coverage. The Germans treat pensioners with a generosity that might evoke the envy of our senior citizens, if the media didn't protect them from information so subversive. A Belgian can collect unemployment compensation indefinitely. Even after four years of Mrs. Thatcher's "free market" governance, an unemployed Briton continues to be covered by the British Health Service and to collect unemployment pay for a full year. To finance such arrangements, Europeans pay far more taxes than do Americans.

These facts make American revulsion against our welfare state —not only Aid to Families with Dependent Children (AFDC) but also pensions, Food Stamps, child nutrition programs, compensatory education, Medicare, Medicaid, and any other transfer of cash or services to the more vulnerable members of society— puzzling. By world standards, these transfers are meager and their tax costs small. Yet the debate over the limits of social policy antedates the arrival of the Reagan administration. The far right has long stigmatized protections against indigence in old age, catastrophic illness, and unemployment as constraints upon personal liberty. More interesting, however, has been the neoconservative assault on the welfare state in journals like *Commentary* and *The Public Interest*. Their contributors stress the sheer fiscal burdens of welfare and still more the rate at which entitlement programs have risen each year since the 1960s. But their concerns go beyond dollars and cents. They assert the superiority of free market devices over bureaucratic arrangements in the delivery of social benefits. Although important distinctions must be made between archaic individualists and sophisticated neoconservatives, the two groups agree that entitlement programs ought to and can be curbed while shielding the poorest from utter destitution.

The Reagan administration in its first year made the severest cuts in social spending in our history, and then justified this by citing a deficit crisis of its own creation. The last Carter deficit, for the fiscal year ending September 30, 1981, was a modest $58 billion. The 1982 deficit—$110 billion—nearly doubled that figure. The estimates for succeeding years start with $207.7 billion as the midyear guess for 1983, proceed to 1984's $188.8 billion, 1985's $194.2 billion, and conclude with 1986's $147.7 billion.[1] In the absence of corrective action, Office of Management and Budget (OMB) director David Stockman and Council of Economic Advisers chairman Martin Feldstein agree that by 1988 the deficit may reach $300 billion. The 1982–1986 projections record the five largest national deficits on record.

The origins of these estimates are familiar. On the expenditure side are the administration's frenzied calls for annual 10 percent enlargements of the military budget *after inflation*, from 1983's $245.5 billion to approximately $380 billion in 1986.[2] Students of the Pentagon judge these estimates as far too low. There is no reason to anticipate smaller cost overruns in the militaristic Reagan administration than in the past, and these are likely to account for a larger fraction of the military budget.

On the revenue side, a terrorized Congress in August, 1981 took a series of mischievous actions[3] certain to cause long-term trouble for the Treasury. The best publicized was a reduction in personal income taxes which, by July of 1983, had lowered effective rates by 25 percent. For average tax filers, the gains are trivial. But citizens whose earnings exceed $200,000 can look forward to average tax savings each year in the 1982–1984 period of $60,000.[4]

Less visible were a series of revisions in business taxation certain to reduce further the corporate share of federal taxes. In 1953, corporate taxes amounted to 30 percent of federal revenues. Administrations of both parties sliced that percentage to 12.5 in 1980. Congressional acceptance in 1981 of administration proposals and the addition of several others halved that number. Corporations now contribute a trifle more than 6 percent to Treasury receipts. In 1981, banks surrendered in taxes a mere 2.7 percent of their earnings.[5]

Congress compounds its indulgence of the wealthy by opening new loopholes and preserving the old ones. Retiring Congressman Henry Reuss released late in 1982 an analysis of the tax indulgences enjoyed by enterprises and individuals. These totaled an annual Treasury loss of $156.6 billion. The usual suspects reaped the bulk of the tax harvest. Here is Reuss's summary:

> Some large tax expenditures have exceedingly regressive impacts on our tax system. Taxpayers with adjusted gross income over $50,000 are 4.4 percent of all taxpayers, receive 19 percent of adjusted gross income, and account for 32.9 percent of taxes after credits. But this same group accounts for:
> - 94 percent of the $4.6 billion tax expenditures from the exclusion of interest on state and local bonds
> - 64 percent of the $13.2 billion revenue loss arising from capital gains, excluding gains from home sales
> - 47 percent of the $17.8 billion tax expenditures due to the deductibility of nonbusiness state and local taxes.[6]

As though to insure a permanent deficit, Congress indexed personal income tax brackets to the inflation rate, starting in 1985. In combination with the reduction of the top rate from 70 to 50 percent and liberalized handling of capital gains, this action dangerously reduced revenue possibilities for the foreseeable future.

Economic forecasting is, to say the least, an imperfect science. Half the recent deficits are a direct result of the recession that administration fiscal and Federal Reserve monetary policies combined to create. In reliability, economic forecasting no doubt improves on astrology but registers error rates higher than meteorology. Early in 1983, as a fair example, the very Martin Feldstein whose *Economic Report of the President* predicted a minute growth rate of 1.4 percent for 1983, a few days later raised his estimate to 3.1 percent, while graciously conceding that a wholesome 5 percent was a genuine possibility. Moreover, the administration presupposes rates of unemployment—over 10 percent in 1983, 9 percent in 1984, and "full" 6.5 percent unemployment by 1987 or 1988[7]—which, one hopes, are politically intolerable for this administration.

A small, far from unreasonable alteration in unemployment assumptions reduces deficit obesity reassuringly. If 1983's unemployment had been 4 percent—the number mandated by the

Humphrey-Hawkins Full Employment and Balanced Growth Act of 1978—the deficit would practically have disappeared. Each dip in unemployment of 1 percent reduces the federal deficit by approximately $30 billion.[8] Six times $30 billion—$180 billion—is $10–20 billion less than the $200 billion 1983 deficit. It follows that persistent operation of the American economy at 4 percent unemployment or less would trash the dreary speculations of administration economists.

Some of the budget deficits, actual and prospective, are the tainted fruit of massive subsidies to the Pentagon and tax cuts almost as imprudent as they are unfair. But the bulk of Treasury shortfalls is the direct, foreseeable corollary of a national failure to insist upon the primacy of jobs during the Ford, Carter, and Reagan administrations. Reagan has done worse than his predecessors because his "supply-side" tax cuts utterly failed to deliver a promised investment boom and, instead, so terrified financial types that interest rates soared to unprecedented heights. The impact upon housing and auto sales was devastating. The same Reagan staffers who in 1981 had been egging on the Federal Reserve to curtail credit, were reduced by the summer of 1982 to pleading for the Fed to reverse its policy and reminding skeptics that Paul Volcker had been appointed by Jimmy Carter.[9]

Social progress is *not* foreclosed because funds are unavailable. As Gordon Adams demonstrates in this volume, elimination of the wilder items in the Pentagon science-fiction catalogue would save some money immediately and vastly more in weapons' cost overruns in the next few years. There are several excellent reasons why the United States can well afford the costs of social progress up to Western European levels. A reasonable approximation of full employment will dramatically enlarge the Gross National Product available for public and private purposes. Substantial sums can be extracted from the Pentagon and even larger amounts from egalitarian tax reform. Finally, as I shall suggest, any agreed-upon, prudent defense effort can be financed more cheaply within the context of national planning—a conclusion equally applicable to the health sector.

If I remain for the time being within the boundaries of ortho-
dox liberalism (I plan soon to escape), I note still another unnecessary restraint upon progress: the existence of the ostensibly
independent Federal Reserve.[10] Although since the summer of
1982 the Fed has reverted to its customary monitoring of interest
rates and other indicators of economic health, the damage that
Paul Volcker and his accomplices have inflicted upon the economy in the preceding three years includes interest extortions at
old-time Mafia levels, blighted consumer markets, bankrupted
farmers and small businessmen, curtailed investment in equipment and factories, even sharper reductions in resources con-
signed to the improvement of human capital—education, health
care, and social services—and a substantial enlargement of the
interest component in the federal budget. In mid-1983, twelve
percent of federal outlays flowed to the holders of public debt,
an amount larger than that allocated to states and localities.[11]

Foreigners have difficulty in understanding why monetary
policy, a major tool of economic management, is shielded from
the direct political control of presidents and Congresses. In England and most other countries, the Chancellor of the Exchequer
or his equivalent issues instructions to the Bank of England or
its analogues. Little more is needed to transform an intolerable
situation than statutory redefinition of the Federal Reserve's role.
As in Britain, the President or his Treasury Secretary might be
empowered to set mandatory interest-rate or money-growth targets. Or Congress could reserve this authority for itself.

By staying with traditional liberalism a bit longer, I can also
demonstrate that the Social Security "crisis" is a fake. On worst-
case assumptions, cumulative deficits in the main Social Security
trust fund *before* Congress "rescued" it early in 1983 approximated $150–200 billion for the remainder of this decade, in an
economy approaching a $3.5 trillion Gross National Product. As
unemployment shrinks, so does the deficit. Whatever remains of
it at lower levels of joblessness is easily handled by drawing upon
general tax revenues—common practice in Western Europe. I
suspect that much of the pother over Social Security and Medicare insolvency cloaks an agenda which includes old-fashioned

conservative resentment of Social Security as an erosion of "individualism" as well as neoconservative arguments that "prove" how much Social Security diminishes private saving, raises interest rates, and dampens business investment.

Tax reform is a frustrated liberal passion. As a result of 1981 and 1982 tax changes and benefit cuts, families with incomes under $10,000 stood to lose $5.8 billion in 1983, $6.1 billion in 1984, and $4.9 billion in 1985. Their economic betters, families drawing down $80,000 or more, were likely to gain (in those three years, respectively) $14.4 billion, $19.0 billion, and $22.2 billion.[12] Loopholes? There are more than ever, crying to be closed.

If the United States really can afford to order a traditional liberal menu—renewed economic growth, tax reform, high employment, comprehensive health coverage, and renewed warfare against poverty—why do old school liberals like Tip O'Neill and Edward Kennedy often seem so lonely? Why do "neoliberals" like Gary Hart and Bill Bradley drop full employment and comprehensive health protection from their immediate priorities? Why do they hare off after Felix Rohatyn's revived Reconstruction Finance Corporation? Why has the Humphrey-Hawkins Balanced Growth and Full Employment Act plummeted down the national memory hole?

Part of the answer is a distortion of political history: the national myth that even at the height of the Great Society we devoted many resources to the alleviation of poverty or seriously endeavored to diminish inequalities of income and wealth. The more interesting explanation of the skittishness of Democratic liberals in Congress focuses upon the tendency of inflation to revive long before full employment by the older, pre-Feldstein criteria is approximated. In the concentrated sectors of the economy—much of manufacturing, insurance, and construction— price setters raise prices and widen profit margins at the first stirrings of economic revival. In the health industry, inflation has not paused even during our two most recent minidepressions, 1974–1975 and 1981–1982. Many or most Democrats fear that serious pursuit of traditional liberal objectives by traditional liberal techniques will then fall prey to cost explosions and dangerous inflation. They are right. The uncomfortable choice before them is between preserving liberal techniques and abandoning liberal objectives or adhering to the objectives and finding new techniques.

The instinct of politicians faced with dangerous choices is to change the subject. For—let there be no mistake—completion of a modern welfare state, high levels of employment, and reasonably stable prices require deliberate national planning (see Michael Harrington's essay in this volume), redistributive taxation in the direction of equality, and public controls over capital movements and corporate pricing policy. All of these policies possess ample precedent in Western Europe, Scandinavia, and Japan. In American terms, they are undeniably radical, and it is the judgment of politicians in this decade that it is suicidal to invite identification as a radical.

But times change. American politics are volatile. I shall sketch in these pages a quite mild radical program, in the belief that it is far from Utopian, fiscally prudent, and responsive to the accumulating needs of middle-class and working-class Americans.

At the top of radical priorities is job creation. In 1983, Congress made a small gesture in this direction by enacting a $4.6 billion program, the most that President Reagan would accept. In the days that men and women blessed with social imagination, the likes of Harry Hopkins and Frances Perkins, actually had the ears of a president, it was possible to find useful work for people desperate to perform it. This was done with a speed hard to comprehend when, as in our day, months and years elapsed without constructive response. Elsewhere in this volume, Bob Kuttner deals at length with the problem of jobs. Here I offer a few marginal notes, necessitated by the simple fact that full employment is the only context within which social progress is probable.

The first concerns cost. In February, 1983, the AFL-CIO Executive Council proposed that the government allocate $22.5 billion for the remainder of that year and $46 billion more in 1984 for a variety of job-creating initiatives, among them training, health care for the unemployed, public works, community development, and housing. To its credit, the Council also supported a trimmed Pentagon budget, a touchy topic for union members dependent on weapons procurement for their jobs.

Expenditures of this size could generate directly 3 million new jobs and an additional number from the repercussions of increased spending by the newly employed throughout the economy. To cut unemployment virtually in half, then, requires relatively trivial extra outlays in a federal budget approximately $850 billion in size. Each additional 1 percent of unemployment translates into $70 billion of Gross National Product, plus the already cited $25–30 billion improvement in Treasury finances flowing from smaller benefits to the unemployed and larger tax collections from the newly employed. As even a cost-benefit *maven* might reluctantly agree, this seems to be a bargain.

My second marginal note concerns the again fashionable theme of public education. In the 1930s, many of the unemployed were utterly or functionally illiterate. Honest observers disagree over the extent of improvement half a century and a Sputnik scare have brought. From grade to graduate school, teachers rarely glow with optimism about verbal and mathematical performance. As usual, these frequently exaggerated inadequacies have evoked cries to return to the "basics." It is all to the good that, as American Federation of Teachers' president Albert Shanker summarized the furor, "there are many different proposals—from the National Commission on Excellence in Education, from the California Round Table, from the National Task Force on Education and Economic Growth, from a task force put together by the Twentieth Century Fund."[13] Still better news is that the signers of these various proclamations recognize that better instruction in reading, writing, science, and mathematics requires more money for high-quality recruits to teaching staffs. In a better society it will be the human services, preeminent among them education, that will supply new jobs—not the will-o'-the-wisp of high technology.

My last marginal note recalls the powerful theme of public-sector deprivation, which John Kenneth Galbraith enunciated a generation ago. He pointed to the contrast between public squalor and private affluence (in 1983 the former is more glaring and the latter more outrageous than in 1958):

> The family which takes its mauve and cerise, air-conditioned, power-steered, and power-braked automobile out for a tour passes through cities that are badly paved, made hideous by litter, blighted buildings, billboards, and posts for wires that should long since have been put underground. They pass on into a countryside that has been rendered largely invisible by commercial art. . . . They picnic on exquisitely packaged food from a portable icebox by a polluted stream and go on to spend the night at a park which is a menace to public health and morals. Just before dozing off on an air mattress, beneath a nylon tent, amid the stench of decaying refuse, they may reflect vaguely on the curious unevenness of their blessings. Is this, indeed, the American genius?[14]

The details have changed; the contrast is sharper than ever. Bridges, roads, sewers, water mains, subways, and buses have deteriorated to an extent menacing to personal safety and to the economic viability of older cities. By one conservative estimate,[15] New York City requires $40 billion in capital improvements over the next few years. As in New York, so in the other battered cities of the Northeast and Midwest.

Old remedies work because old problems recur. As in the 1930s, the human labor to do the repairs is abundant. Now as then, much of the work can be performed by the so-called structurally unemployed, once genuine national commitment to full employment becomes reality.

Full employment is not only the prerequisite of social advance, it is in itself a radical objective. Its absence erodes the already reduced influence of organized labor. In the early years of this decade, unions threatened by layoffs and plant closings in the steel, auto, railroad, meatpacking, and airline industries have agreed to eliminate "unneeded jobs" and to redefine remaining jobs by "adding duties." In automaking, rubber, steel, petroleum, and construction, unions have combined such craft jobs as millwright, welder, rigger, and boilermaker. In at least seven industries, unions have given up relief and wash-up periods, agreed to work more hours for the same pay, and allowed management "more flexibility in scheduling daily and weekly hours." Similar concessions applying to seniority and incentive pay have been common.[16] Many American managers, never willing to accept unions, have seized upon economic crisis to weaken if not destroy their adversaries.

Full employment, accordingly, is as menacing to corporate power as its absence is to workers. It would shift economic leverage from the corporate sector to unions and their political allies. If, in the context of full employment, a rising percentage of the labor force is publicly employed, then worker dependence upon private employers diminishes and the latter must bid for workers instead of the other way around. Structural unemployment then diminishes as employers hire and train allegedly hard-core types, much as they did during World War II.

Effective pursuit of high employment demands control of capital movements. As a start, tax incentives that now stimulate export of domestic capital to other countries must be eliminated. Unrepatriated profits should be taxed as though transferred to the United States in the year actually earned. Once under political control, the Federal Reserve ought to discourage loans to authoritarian regimes and the American multinationals that collaborate with them. The agency should allocate credit on preferential terms to family farmers, small businessmen, community-based Health Maintenance Organizations and energy cooperatives, and not-for-profit housing ventures. Limitations on plant closings ought to include substantial financial penalties upon solvent enterprises that plan to resume operations elsewhere. Generous severance pay and tax indemnities to deserted communities would block many plans to move to antiunion, low-wage havens.

Such proposals will evoke foreseeable outrage from the business media. In Western Europe, they are routine policies to which subsidiaries of American corporations accommodate themselves. The American market is much too large to be deserted by multinationals in a fury at policies commonplace in countries less indulgent of large corporations.

I come to a final consequence of full employment: it is likely to be inflationary. As less efficient men and women are pulled into the labor force, productivity declines, labor costs rise, prices are marked up, unions play catch-up, a second round of price hikes ensues, and so on. There is *something* in this conventional line of analysis; but it notably fails to explain why prices begin to stir ominously early in typical recoveries from recession, months or years before the "structurally" unemployed are enrolled in the labor force.

As ever, standard economics overlooks the obvious. The American economy is half competitive (to be generous) and half administered by dominant sellers. In 1981, 1982, and 1983—their three worst years since the 1930s—steel and auto companies steadily *raised* prices. This is very different from the response of Seventh Avenue garment manufacturers to unsold inventory: they run sales. General Motors and United States Steel can choose between high price–low volume and low price–high volume as ways of responding to shrinking sales and rebellious customers. Almost always, at the first intimation of recovery, they tend to shove prices still higher, even though many of their facilities are still underutilized and thousands of workers on indefinite layoff. No need to impose price controls on the rag merchants, urban supermarkets, and retailing in general. There, competition is real. But controls are urgent wherever economic power is concentrated in a small number of corporate hands. Such is the situation in much of manufacturing, banking and insurance, and health services.

Genetic engineering recombines existing genetic elements to generate new plant varieties and—in time, conceivably—new men and women. Full employment, nationalization, and controls are familiar policy instruments. Nevertheless, the particular combination of initiatives that I favor is, for this country, a radical departure from traditional reliance upon private-sector solutions and the traditional distrust of government which is its corollary.

Can the United States afford full employment, universal health protection, and adequate national defense? I have already foreshadowed an affirmative answer. Full employment, of course, is not free. It does not do to underestimate the size of needed enlargements of our national outlays on education, training, public jobs, housing, and capital commitments to urban infrastructures. But these ought to be compared to an array of costs due to persistent high unemployment, such as transfer payments to the unemployed, Food Stamps, Medicaid, welfare, and unemployment compensation. In subsequent years, unemployment will be reflected in mental and physical illness, suicide, family disruption, child abuse, and crime. As intelligent moderates and conservatives from Edmund Burke through Benjamin Disraeli to Felix Rohatyn have recognized, social disorganization costs respectable people money sooner or later. It is also bad for business.

The financing of full employment in the short run can draw upon the closing of tax loopholes and the restoration of progressivity in the personal income tax. Up to $50 billion in additional revenue can quite plausibly be raised. In the longer run, the enhanced productivity and renewed growth of an economy operating at full capacity will yield—even at existing tax rates—almost enough to balance annual budgets.

What I have said is, of course, familiar liberal prescription and good as far as it goes. But there is a further, less familiar point to be made. Even in financial terms, radical institutional reform is potentially thriftier than either liberal or conservative tinkering.

Two important examples of radical saving are the defense and health sectors of the economy. It is likely that the political pressures that have prevented congresspeople from axing even useless weapons' systems will diminish in a climate of high employment. When unemployment is high, the same members of Congress who endorse nuclear freezes lobby to get New York, Boston, or Newport designated as home port for recommissioned World War II battleships armed with cruise missiles.

The Pentagon has astutely spread defense business across the country, in practically every congressional district. A few strategically placed telephone calls to bankers, merchants, and local union officials can whip up opposition to budget limitations overnight. Even in an atmosphere of high or full employment, this coalition will be troublesome.

There is an additional institutional arrangement, also terribly expensive, that is more open to remedy. I allude to the relationship between large defense contractors and the Pentagon. In all but legal form, Grumman, General Dynamics, Boeing, and a handful of their peers are subsidiaries of the Pentagon. A very large percentage of contracts is negotiated without competitive bidding to this tight brotherhood. A new weapon dreamed up by a defense contractor may enlarge the domain of high Pentagon officials. Rival weapons proposed by other contractors can win Pentagon endorsement and congressional funding. While they are still in uniform, generals will preside over growing budgets and larger cohorts of subordinates; upon retirement, lucrative posts await them with grateful weapons' merchants. It would take a fool or a saint to deal harshly with a potential employer.

Even if competitive bidding were the rule and high officers in retirement honorably avoided defense-related employment, waste would be generated by frictions between these two huge and basically cooperative bureaucracies—the military and the corporate. Haggling between them delays design decisions, multiplies the number of reviewing authorities, encourages midcourse alterations, stretches out procurement, and adds enormously to the cost overruns in this inefficient sector of the American economy.

The world is a dangerous place. In the foreseeable future, total disarmament is fantasy, but adequate national defense can be financed much less wastefully. John Kenneth Galbraith has cogently argued for a version of nationalization:

> The combined power of the two bureaucracies would be usefully reduced by converting the large specialized weapons firms into full public corporations. . . . The government would acquire their stock at recently prevailing stock market valuation. Thereafter the boards of directors and senior management would be appointed by the federal government. Salaries and other emoluments would henceforth be regulated by the government in general relation to public levels; profits would accrue to the government; so also would losses as is now the case.[17]

As Galbraith adds, large contractors already do most of their business with government, collect working capital and progress payments from the Pentagon, and use large quantities of plant and equipment owned by that agency. The government absorbs losses and, as with Lockheed, trots to the rescue when bankruptcy threatens.

Let us, accordingly, diminish the number of bureaucracies. Between corporate and public bureaucracy, there are reasons to prefer the latter. Its managers come cheaper. Their motives are less exploitative. Congress and the media habitually oversee the actions of government with more enthusiasm and less pressure from campaign contributors than they do those of private corporations.

But the most spectacular opportunities for radical thrift are to be found in the health sector. The position of the medical profession in the United States seems to be unique in the modern world. Doctors have preserved substantial professional autonomy from both government and big business. Physicians cling to a model of small entrepreneurial organization[18] in a period when universities, law and accounting firms, and newspaper chains have succumbed to corporate bureaucracy. Even though private health insurers—Blue Cross and others—and federal and local governments pay most of their bills, doctors retain potent influence over fee schedules, hospital care, hospital attending privileges, and so on.

Public and government insistence upon cost limitations have begun to diminish the power of health providers to compel others to pay for services to patients at prices determined by physicians and hospitals. The market-oriented Reagan strategy emphasizes two innovations, the first a ceiling of $2,100 on tax-exempt employer contributions to health insurance covering an employee and his or her family and an $840 cap for an individual employee. The second allows Medicare recipients to substitute for Medicare protection a voucher tradeable for private insurance coverage. The administration also favors "prospective payment" to hospitals by "diagnosis-related groups." Efficient hospitals will be permitted to keep the money they make. Less well-managed hospitals will be compelled to absorb outlays in excess of prospective reimbursement. The administration proposal most likely to result in immediate savings increases the share of hospital costs to be borne by the elderly. Free market strategies start with the assumption that the market for health services is much like other markets. With competition, suppliers will improve efficiency, the better to maximize profit. Compelled to bear a larger share of health costs, union members, corporate employers, and the elderly will shop more carefully for the best bargains and allow minor ailments to cure themselves.

Unfortunately, the health market really is different from normal commerce in securities, vacation packages, and groceries. Its closest analogue appears to be the funeral business. When any supplier—physician or funeral director—holds customers captive, he controls both sides of the transaction. It is the doctor, not the apprehensive patient, who composes the medical menu. No wonder health is an expensive and elusive commodity. In 1929, its purveyors collected 4 percent of the Gross National Product. In 1970 the percentage was 7.3, and 9.4 percent a decade later. In 1983, it was rising toward 11 percent. So far in this decade, the price of health care has escalated at a rate two to three times that of inflation in general.

Yet, by the end of the 1980s, a burgeoning surplus of physicians threatens a ratio of population to doctors akin to that in Israel. In a competitive market, surpluses would drive prices down. Competition in health care, however, tends to drive costs higher instead of lower. Not only may physicians impose unnecessary costs upon patients as the number of the latter diminishes, but hospitals also play the game. Hospital administrators compete for physician favor by installing the latest in medical technology, even if it duplicates existing facilities in nearby hospitals. Early in 1983, two hospitals in Columbia, Missouri (population 65,000) were seeking approval to acquire still experimental X-ray equipment costing several million dollars.

In ordinary markets, astute merchants profit from segmenting their customers and concentrating upon the most affluent. Corporations engaged in for-profit health care pursue their own variant on this technique. Major operators like Humana and National Health Care acquire and operate chains of hospitals and dialysis centers on "sound" commercial principles. These naturally include avoidance of low-income, elderly, and chronically ailing patients. The young are gratifyingly prey to severe illnesses that require lucrative but brief surgical interventions and hospital stays. For several decades, their incomes will rise and their children comprise a second generation of customers. Meanwhile in urban America, fewer and fewer residents can claim their own family physician; emergency rooms[19] in voluntary hospitals divert the medically indigent to municipal hospitals; and health delivery seems poised to return to the two-track system from which Great Society legislation temporarily rescued it —good care for the middle classes and the rich, cheap and inferior care for the poor.

In short, health providers have, at intolerable financial cost, ill served the vulnerable and disappointed the prosperous. The situation, worse now, was serious enough to alert *Business Week* as far back as 1970. Its judgment deserves quotation:

> Most of U.S. medical care, particularly the everyday business of preventing and treating routine illnesses, is inferior in quality, wastefully dispensed, and inequitably financed. Medical manpower and facilities are so maldistributed that large segments of the population, especially the urban poor and those in rural areas, get virtually no care at all—even though their illnesses are most numerous and in a medical sense, often easy to cure. Whether poor or not, most Americans are badly served by the obsolete, overstrained medical system that has grown up around them helter skelter . . . *the time has come for radical change.* [Italics added.] [20]

Celebrants of market capitalism routinely claim that it maximizes both efficiency and freedom of consumer choice. For nonmedical markets, the celebration is loudest on the part of the winners. In the medical marketplace, there are more losers than winners, notably the unemployed and their families, pensioners, and the working poor. For all parties, American health care is painfully expensive.

But other societies cope with health costs more sensibly. The British Health Service, for example, costs taxpayers 5.5 percent of a per capita Gross National Product less than half our own. After a half-decade of Conservative financial starvation, its imperfections are serious and numerous. Yet "of ten Western countries, the U.S. was second in spending but ninth in health; Britain was last in spending, fourth in health."[21] North of our border, the Canadians operate a system somewhere between the British salaried service and the American entrepreneurial model. It involves fees and hospital charges negotiated between government and health providers, at a cost of 7.5–8.0 percent of Gross National Product. While considerably cheaper than the American product, the Canadian system offers comprehensive coverage.

To many observers, national health, like antitrust enforcement and equitable tax reform, is just one more lost cause. Franklin Roosevelt rejected health protection in the 1935 Social Security Act. After 1948, Harry Truman got precisely nowhere in renewed advocacy. For an instant during the Nixon era, a conservative version seemed politically feasible; the moment passed. As a candidate desperate for Automobile Workers' endorsement, Jimmy Carter pledged priority for comprehensive coverage. Instead he opted for welfare reform, which Congress contemptuously rejected.

In Reagan's wake, nevertheless, the elusive goal may be reached, either as an echo of the British salaried service or the Canadian public-private negotiated compromise, an extension of Health Maintenance Organizations, or a mixture of these elements. In spite of frequent sabotage from organized medicine, Health Maintenance Organizations have a good record of reducing hospitalization rates and curtailing average hospitalization stays. Their success and that of state services elsewhere in the world raises the possibility of an effective coalition for universal health protection. Its members might include ordinary middle-class families disaffected by the cost of incomplete care; large employers exercised by steeper Blue Cross-Blue Shield premiums paid on behalf of employees and their dependents; cities that must pay for the poor; and (strategically crucial) a large, annually increasing cadre of young doctors menaced by diminishing patient pools, heavy educational debts, the huge costs of solo practice, and barriers erected by established, older doctors against admission to hospital practice.

For new doctors, the choice often is not between private and salaried medical practice; it is between the Humana and the public payroll. To a degree, the entrepreneurial drive of doctors has been ameliorated by the tradition of altruism toward the helpless. That altruism is far less likely to be fostered in corporate than in public environments. To maximizers of bottom lines in corporate medicine, poor people are of no interest except as burdens to be avoided. Established doctors will no doubt cling to the entrepreneurial independence that has rewarded them lavishly. But their interests and those of younger colleagues already diverge and shortly will diverge still more widely.

In what one hopes will be the more progressive political climate of 1985 and after, it is unlikely that the American Medical Association (to which less than half the country's M.D.'s belong) will be able credibly to present itself as the single voice of American medicine. Haters of inequity and enemies of inefficiency may join hands in the creation of a superior system of health delivery.

In 1980, Americans tacitly agreed to trade equity for efficiency, faster economic growth, and rising living standards. It was a bad bargain. The impact of assaults upon programs for low-income Americans has been amply documented. So has the effect of 1981's tax legislation on the relative fortunes of rich, middle-class, and low-income families. The administration has played favorites even among its own business clients. Commercial banks, transportation enterprises, shipbuilders, and railroads pay negative taxes as a result of special legislative favors. Aerospace producers pay at the rate of 13.5 percent, but publishers and printers at nearly triple that figure. Even the rich have cause to complain.[22]

The ill-assorted trio of supply-side tax incentives, tight money, and massive weapons procurement generated not economic growth but severe unemployment and, instead of rising living standards, deterioration in the real incomes of blue-collar and white-collar workers. Homes and farms have been foreclosed on, and small businesses have filed for bankruptcy in numbers unprecedented since the Great Depression. By the test of the market, supposedly venerated by Reagan economists, Reagan policies have failed.

In the next few years, political debate will focus on alternative paths to prosperity. Public perception that Great Society liberalism has reached a dead end is, in my view, accurate. It is too expensive to continue bribing doctors, hospitals, developers, construction unions, and other entrenched suppliers to stop hindering Medicare, Medicaid, and low-income housing. Still, the list of failed industries should give pause to admirers of corporate America. In addition to steel, autos, housing, and health, there is the issue of nuclear power. New plants are prodigiously expensive. Waste disposal is an unresolved problem. Evidence mounts that nuclear accidents have been more frequent than public exposure of their occurrence. In Washington, voters have blocked further nuclear construction. On Long Island, the Shoreham nuclear plant will, by some measures, cost taxpayers more if it is allowed to open than if it is junked as a multibillion-dollar blunder.

If major money market bankers—Citibank, Chase, Morgan Guaranty, Chemical, Bankers Trust, and Manufacturers Hanover—were compelled to value accurately all their dubious loans at home and abroad, they would be insolvent. Their continuation as apparently solvent institutions testifies partly to the political clout of the industry and, for the rest, to fear that a major banking bankruptcy would precipitate a global financial panic.

It is already apparent that the response of intelligent conservatives and moderate liberals is to shore up major operators in the corporate sector by some version of "industrial policy." This vague term comprehends proposals like Felix Rohatyn's revived Reconstruction Finance Corporation, Robert Reich's tax incentives and tax penalties to encourage investment in productive directions, and Bennett Harrison's and Barry Bluestone's anti-plant-closing strategies.[23] *Business Week* has floated a careful version of indicative planning that called for business-union partnership blessed by government.

These proposals share an inclination to guide investment and a preference for tax and credit tools of policy. With the exception of Harrison and Bluestone, industrial policy advocates put their bets on the same corporate community whose defects have been the source of unsatisfactory economic performance for a decade and a half Even the most liberal version of industrial policy, that of Robert Reich, defines the corporate role as central.

There is reason to be skeptical of this outlook. Industrial policy has served leading Democrats as an excuse to avoid discussions of health care, full employment, urban revival, and adequate housing. Still, on present indications, it is likely to be at the center of political debate.

Industrial policy is probably preferable to Reaganomics. (Almost any change would represent improvement.) However, it ought not to be confused with full employment, democratic planning, or a fair redistribution of the nation's income and wealth. Progress on these fronts demands strategies considerably more radical than subsidies to business that are better targeted than usual.[24] It requires an expanded welfare state, that is, more rather than less government participation in the actual production of weapons, energy, housing, and health services; political control of monetary policy; overhaul of the tax code; and effective incomes policy. Above all, once again, radical policy must start with full employment.

Democrats have retreated from full employment as an objective much as they have quietly shelved other items on the party agenda since the New Deal—health, housing, and tax reform. As a cure for American economic troubles, industrial policy— the apparent alternative policy—is delusive. High-tech industries promise at best to generate comparatively small numbers of jobs, many as unskilled as those in traditional industries. No doubt better business leadership and improved public policy can potentially revive American manufacturing. But the fact is that the unfilled needs of Americans are, for the most part, of a kind that demands improvement in human services—education, training, nursing care, counseling, and recreation.

Industrial policy is a confused political cry. Moreover, even if a Democrat does succeed Ronald Reagan, he will find himself frustrated by the same resource limitations that constrain the Democratic opposition in Congress at the moment. This is to say once more that, under current institutional arrangements, the American welfare state, rickety as it was at the end of Jimmy Carter's term, is still too expensive for an economy operating far below its capacity. Drastic institutional change is essential to the retention even of existing social programs, let alone equitable improvement in them. Our version of market capitalism has developed flaws more serious for many Americans than inequity —flaws such as inefficiency, health menaces, defective quality, falling educational performance, and incomplete health protection even for the middle class.

I have not here considered the political feasibility of the changes which I have proposed. The need for them is plain, however elusive at this time may be the political will to take radical action. One must wonder, all the same, about the viability of a Democratic opposition that accepts so much of its opponents' case and exhibits such extreme programmatic timidity. In the absence of radical change, the Democratic party—and, far more important, American society—will continue to decline in equity, efficiency, and opportunity.

As for 1983's recovery, it is naturally welcome; but its very limited impact upon unemployment reveals the persistent weaknesses of our economy and the undiminished urgency of radical approaches to their alleviation.

NOTES

1. *See The United States Budget in Brief: Fiscal Year 1984*, Office of Management and Budget, 27. *See also The Economic Report of the President*, February 1983, 26–28; and *Report* of the Joint Economic Committee, 98th Cong., 1st Sess., S. Rept. 98-115.
2. *See The United States Budget in Brief: Fiscal Year 1984*, 33–34.
3. Just a year later, Congress clawed back some of the more egregious tax breaks lavished upon corporations and affluent individuals.
4. *Growth with Fairness: Progressive Economic Policies for the Eighties*, ed. Robert S. McIntyre (The Institute on Taxation and Economic Policy), 2.
5. AFL-CIO News, April 2, 1983, 2.

6. Joint Economic Committee Press Release, November 20, 1982, 1.

7. *See* the *Economic Report of the President,* February 1983, 144.

8. *See* the Op-Ed page of *New York Times,* February 8, 1983.

9. At the risk of dancing upon the grave of Reaganomics, I do take modest pride in my early celebration of the funeral rites. My *Greed Is Not Enough: Reaganomics* appeared in January 1982. It was written in the summer of 1981, early in the career of the Reagan follies.

10. "Ostensibly" is the right word. In the summer of 1972, then Federal Reserve chairman Arthur F. Burns obligingly eased credit and pumped up the economy in the interests of his patron Richard Nixon. Ten years later, Paul Volcker junked a three-year-old experiment in monetarism just in time to limit Republican losses in the 1982 congressional elections.

11. *See The United States Budget in Brief, Fiscal Year 1984,* 1.

12. Congressional Budget Office, *Effects of Tax and Benefit Reductions Enacted in 1981 for Households in Different Income Categories,* February 1982, 4, 25.

13. Albert Shanker, "Where We Stand," *New York Times,* May 8, 1983.

14. *See* John Kenneth Galbraith, *The Affluent Society* (Boston: Houghton Mifflin Co., 1976), 253.

15. That of David Grossman, head of the NOVA Foundation and a former Budget Director of the City of New York.

16. I have relied upon an approving *Business Week* cover story, "A Work Revolution in U. S. Industry," May 16, 1983, 100.

17. John Kenneth Galbraith, *Economics and the Public Purpose* (Boston: Houghton Mifflin Co., 1973), 284.

18. In much of the following discussion, I rely on Paul Starr's valuable *The Social Transformation of American Medicine* (New York: Basic Books, 1983) and Bennett Harrison and Barry Bluestone, *Deindustrial-Republic,* April 18, 1983, 19–23.

19. In New Orleans and a number of other cities, voluntary hospitals are actually closing emergency rooms or curtailing the days and hours they are available.

20. Quoted by Starr, *Social Transformation,* 381.

21. *See,* of all authorities, *Wall Street Journal,* February 9, 1983.

22. *Dun's Business Monthly,* May 1983, 41.

23. *See* Robert Reich, *The Next American Frontier* (New York: Times Books, 1983) and Bennett Harrison and Barry Bluestone, *Deindustrializing America* (New York: Basic Books, 1983).

24. In 1972, the city of Yonkers devoted over $7 million to the acquisition and development of a site for an Otis Elevator Plant. Otis was subsequently acquired by an international conglomerate, United Technologies Corporation, which decided in May of 1983 to close the plant and distribute its production elsewhere. As *The Washington Post* (May 15, 1983) reported the story, Otis noted that "it was a business decision. . . . I don't think it's a moral question." A HUD spokesman also washed his hands: "I do not believe the federal government has any continuing responsibility. . . . It is a local dispute." Yonkers thought it was buying an expanding factory. It wasted its money: a warning to industrial policy advocates.

VI. A CASE
FOR DEMOCRATIC
PLANNING

MICHAEL HARRINGTON

EVERYONE, including those who swear by Adam Smith and Milton Friedman, is for national economic planning. For one thing, America has long since ceased to be anything like a "free market" economy. For another, we are in the midst of a period in which, to use Joseph Schumpeter's phrase, there must be "adjustments to long range and . . . fundamental . . . changes." There is occurring an historic shift in the international division of labor as countries like South Korea and Brazil produce steel more cheaply than Japan and West Germany; an unprecedented internationalization of capital by banks as well as by multinational corporations organizing their "global factories"; and a technological revolution that is already eliminating blue-collar jobs in smokestack industries and is moving into the clerical sector as well. No one proposes to allow these disruptive trends simply to work their will. Everyone is for planning.

Take Ronald Reagan the planner (I summarize and quote from the 1982 and 1983 *Reports* of his Council of Economic Advisors). The administration believes that, in contrast to Europe, the United States neglected to encourage savings and investment in the post–World War II period. We made, it is said, the wrong allocation of capital. Note: it was not the "free market" that, according to the Reaganites, made this error. It was faulty government planning, and the remedy is sound government planning. "The administration seeks to increase capital formation by both raising the level of output and reducing the fraction of output consumed." How? "Household choices between consumption and saving and between work and leisure are influenced by after-tax wage rates and after-tax rates of return on capital. *When the government changes either the level or the structure of taxes*, it ultimately alters household decisions about consumption, saving and work effort." (Emphasis added.)

The sovereign consumer-citizens thus decide how hard to work and how much to save, just as the old faith said they should. But they do so in a context rigged by Washington so that the sovereign choices will produce a planned result. So much for the "free market."

Not so incidentally, the means chosen to increase the pool of savings involved a radical redistribution of wealth from working people and the middle class to the rich. Fair tax cuts for the bottom 95 percent of the society would simply increase consumption (the demand side), while giveaways to the top 5 percent (and, even more pointedly, to the top nine-tenths of one percent who received roughly 17 percent of total benefits) would lead to investment, growth, and reduced deficits. Reagan's shamefaced planning contents itself with manipulating the economy to force it to come up with a pool of savings, but then counts—fecklessly, as it turned out—on financial markets to channel that upwardly mobile money to "sound" uses.

The rich graciously accepted the billions conferred upon them to start an investment boom and promptly put it to speculative uses. That trend was, of course, reinforced by the monetarist component in Reaganomics which followed a suicidal policy that not only subsidized wasteful games with American resources but also helped undermine the European economy.

When a recovery began in 1983, the President claimed that it was the result of his management of the economy. It was nothing of the sort, since the projected investment boom of "supply-side economics" had turned into an investment bust that continued into 1983. There were two reasons why things began to improve: the quiet Keynesian, "demand-side" effect of deficits, and the savage "discipline" imposed upon an economy with 15 million people out of work. Unions were subjected to the most militant corporate attack since Herbert Hoover, which led to wage restraints and concessions; the less profitable factories were shut down even if that destroyed communities; and an industrial plant operating at around two-thirds of capacity helped lower the Consumer Price Index. Creating the worst economic disaster in half a century, we now know, is a way to reduce inflation.

Ronald Reagan, obviously, is not an anti-planner; he is just an incompetent planner. Even though he finally blundered into a partial recovery, the basic structural determinants of our crisis —the new world division of labor, internationalization of capital, and technological revolution—are still very much in force. The planning imperative remains.

But what kind of planning? Will it focus on broad aggregates, like the supply of capital, and deputize decisions on the use of the publicly funded stimulus to the corporate board room? That was what Reaganomics did, and it brought the result we have seen. Or will there be further incoherent and uncoordinated government interventions into the economy, which add up to a sort of unintended "plan"? That happened in the steel industry, where protectionist measures allowed the companies not to modernize but to shift capital to the chemical and oil industries. Or will there be a conscious allocation of resources to specific sectors; and if so, will that be done technocratically, in the "Japanese" style, or democratically?

Democratic planning is not without its dangers and limits. Totalitarian Communist economies provide a dramatic illustration of the threat to human freedom inherent in a bureaucratic, centralist allocation of resources. Such an approach is not simply antithetical to civil liberties; it has also been economically inefficient, characterized by shoddy goods produced in a wasteful fashion. There is, to be sure, no Joseph Stalin waiting in the wings of American politics. But there are decent people with great respect for our political traditions who believe that a truly democratic approach to planning is a contradiction in terms. You cannot, Felix Rohatyn insists, have unruly groups from the base of society intruding upon the technocratic decisions that have to be made from the top. I disagree profoundly, out of a democratic conviction that the planners must be subject to constant and informed criticism, even removal, if a plan is to work.

Nor does a truly democratic planning process guarantee good choices. The French socialists in 1981 did many excellent things —the greatest political decentralization in France since Napoleon, a "solidaristic" incomes policy aimed at helping the lowest paid, a fifth week of vacation, and so on. But they also made a serious error for which they are paying a high political price. They assumed in 1981 and early 1982 that, just as the experts of the capitalist West said, the recession would end after the first quarter of 1982. They were wrong, and that subverted many of their attractive policies.

What does that prove? Does the failure of a new government to master the worst economic crisis in half a century demonstrate that democratic planning won't work? Or that undemocratic planning would have done better? Hardly. It does show that planning is not a panacea, that there will be errors—even serious errors—in the best of plans, and that nonetheless it is the only progressive option for confronting a major shift in the structures of the international economy.

My essay concentrates on details, precisely because details alone will carry adequate conviction of the practicality of our proposals; but it is animated at every point by a larger vision. Ronald Reagan is the apostle of a mean-spirited laissez faire ideology, even while he engages in his shamefaced planning. He is a threat to the American spirit as well as to the American economy. And the point of the alternative to Reagan that I am proposing is that there can be human cooperation, a meaningful reorganization of work as opposed to Reagan's romanticized rat race. I am not suggesting a dreamy voyage into that long run in which, as Keynes said, we are all dead. What is urged here is both relevant to the 1980s *and* a first step toward a different kind of twenty-first century.

There are two related aspects of the democratic planning process with which we begin, a national needs inventory, involving the broadest participation of the people and supplying data for technical proposals to be developed by experts; and a national input-output analysis of the economy based upon a calculus of social efficiency which would use the needs inventory as a basis for industrial policy and full employment planning.

The concept of a national needs inventory is already contained in draft legislation written by Bertram Gross and others for Representative John Conyers. It would involve planning agencies at every level of government in making an "assessment of unmet needs" in such areas as basic environmental resources, housing, high-speed trains, infrastructure, health, education, and community organization and mobilization. It would have short-run concerns—creating a "shelf" of desirable projects, planned in advance, which could provide useful work when required by counter-cyclical policy—as well as long-run goals, like the "rational revitalization of industrial facilities. . . ."

One of the most important features of the Gross-Conyers proposal is that mechanisms would be established to allow local and state governments to involve themselves effectively in the undertaking. Broadly speaking, in a computerized information society, those who define and process the data have enormous power, not least because they can make their own choices look like the dictates of impersonal machines, a version of mathematical necessity. (When David Stockman didn't like the OMB computer's analysis of the 1981 proposals, he simply reprogrammed it until it told him what the President wanted to hear.) At the present time, there are only two entities that have the technical capacity to engage in sophisticated planning (or deception): the federal government and the *Fortune* 500 corporations. If that oligopoly control continues, then all efforts at planning are almost inevitably going to turn into closed-door negotiations between the government and corporate technocrats.

The Gross-Conyers draft rightly suggests that federal funding be made available to local levels of government so that they can establish their priorities in the most effective way. The people at the bottom are, in most cases, much more effective analysts of local needs than the most sophisticated planner in Washington. But they often lack the technical capacity to order their insights in a systematic way or to translate them into the appropriate computer language. They have to be given the ability to hire their experts to controvert, if necessary, the official experts in the federal government.

I would take this idea one step further. Significant minorities, both locally and nationally, should also have the chance to participate effectively in this exercise. Consequently, one imperative of the planning process is to empower all significant groups in the society—not just regional, state, and local governments—with the computer time and the paid experts that are a precondition of any truly democratic planning.

The Gross-Conyers draft suggests creating a Temporary Commission on Democratic Rights and Planning, which would use the data from the needs inventory to formulate "a proposed program of guaranteed opportunities for useful and productive employment." However, although the Gross-Conyers proposal outlines the mechanism for and mandates the goals of full employment planning, it does not get into the actual content of these prospective plans. Indeed, it is something of a paradox, in advance of the democratic determinations of needs, to argue about what they should be. I propose to live with that paradox by simply saying that the ideas I will develop here are ideas that the democratic left would urge *within* that procedure.

First, there must be an industrial policy for the revitalization of "smokestack" America. All those analyses that write off our industrial heartland are not just socially cruel; they are foolish. More often than not, they utterly confuse trends and relative decline with *faits accomplis* and absolute numbers. It is true that manufacturing dropped between 1959 and 1979 from 24.1 percent of total employment to 20.6 percent. And there are projections that envision a further decrease to 19.5 percent in 1990. But a "mere" 20.6 percent of the labor force is more than 20 million men and women (not to mention their collective impact on the communities in which they live). Even if the numbers turn out to be much worse than the current predictions, during the rest of this century, smokestack America is going to be a major source of jobs and wealth, if it is integrated into a useful plan.

Indeed, as UAW analysts have pointed out, the current shift in the international division of labor requires that the U.S. economy emphasize not simply high-tech electronics and bio-technology but industries characterized by high added value per worker: machine tools, heavy equipment, engines and generators, autos, steel, aluminum, aircraft, energy hardware, computers, and telecommunications. The advanced capitalist world typically exports its—routinized—technological revolutions to the peripheral countries. Textiles were the first; steel and ship-building have followed. And so, not so incidentally, have the productive jobs in high-tech industries, as Atari's move to Asia shows.

In fact, a northern—an American—commitment to the modernization of the Third World by transferring wealth and technology from North to South could create a large number of jobs in the North as well as in the South. The agony of the Third World in the current international crisis is not simply terrible for the poor but bad for the semi-affluent of the developed societies as well. An effective investment in greater justice for the world economy would be in the interests of northern workers who could create the hardware for the modernization of the South. The American trade union movement does not often see it that way; but it is nonetheless true. Labor should understand that a pro–Third World policy could be a means precisely of providing a new, and exceedingly useful, lease on life for the traditional industrial sectors. But here again this can only happen as part of a plan.

A final point on the smokestack question. High technology

is not an end in itself: computerized numerical control machines are designed not to be admired, but to be used—and used in producing "medium high-tech" goods, like machine tools, autos, and steel. Unless the proponents of high-tech strategies have become Third World romantics, that is, unless they believe that the Brazilian, South Korean, and Mexican markets are capable of absorbing all of those control machines, they must simultaneously be committed to refurbishing the industrial sector. Otherwise, America will become what Paul Samuelson has called the "cathedral town" of the world economy—a place like those medieval episcopal centers that produced nothing and administered everything.

Another major theme for democratic macro-economic planning: that it utilize input-output analysis to anticipate major economic shifts. Nobel laureate Wassily Leontief was the first to work out the details of input-output analysis—a method that quantifies the interrelations between each sector and industry of an economy and thereby permits one to calculate the global consequences of any given change in one or many sectors. In the September 1982 *Scientific American*, Leontief described how Austrian socialists used input-output techniques to deal with major technological transitions, specifically "to model and project the impact of the new text-processing and printing technologies on the Austrian newspaper industry. That technological revolution, the occasion for months-long disputes and work stoppages in Britain, the United States, and other countries, was carried out smoothly and expeditiously in Austria by close cooperation between management and labor in accordance with detailed plans developed by the government." Not coincidentally, the Austrians were more successful in dealing with inflation and unemployment in the seventies than any other Western country.

This should not be taken to imply that there is a kind of nonpolitical, value-free technical planning that can resolve serious conflicts by computer models. For one thing, the Austrian government was put there by the workers and kept their confidence throughout. That, clearly, is not easily repeated in a

United States in which the working people, though basically Democratic voters, do not regard any party as "their" party.

It is clear, moreover, that all mathematical models—all statistics, for that matter—can be given a social bias. I am not speaking here simply of open-and-shut cases, for example, David Stockman's rigging the computer. More broadly, the corporate concept of efficiency refuses, as far as legally possible, to internalize the social costs of private decisions. There were at least two public dimensions of any investment decision which are thereby omitted: the direct social cost (the $30 billion federal loss for every 1 percent of unemployment; the destruction of the economic basis of political communities; and similar consequences); and the ripple effect as a shutdown ramifies throughout the economy, affecting suppliers, their workers, their communities, and so on.

There is a major difference between private and social planning. Take a simple hypothetical case. A decision has to be taken whether to maintain or shut down a steel mill. From the corporate point of view, there is only one question at issue: not whether that mill is running at a profit or a deficit, but whether the funds tied up in its operation can be invested at a higher rate of return elsewhere. If the answer is "yes," then from this perspective the plant is operating at a "loss," even if it yields a substantial profit. And insofar as they represent no legal obligations—via clauses in the union contract or laws regulating shutdowns—workers and communities profoundly affected by the decision made in the board room simply do not figure into the calculation.

In a *social* calculus—and it barely matters, at this point, whether the plant is publicly owned or private, as long as it functions within the framework of a plan—the methodology and, quite possibly, the decision would be considerably different. If the plant were closed, what would be the immediate impact on government income, both national and local? The cost for unemployment compensation, retraining, lost taxes at every level? The consequence of this shutdown for other businesses in the community and region, and the cost of that to the cities, states, and national government? A mill running at a deficit might be kept open because the overall cost of closing it would actually be higher than the subsidies required to run it. The Swedish *conservative* government came to something like that conclusion when it nationalized a part of the steel industry.

Does this mean that a legislative fiat will decree that buggy-whip factories be kept open in the age of the automobile? Over the long haul, no. In the short run, as a means of coping with the social costs of a wrenching transition, quite possibly. This does not, however, mean that democratic planning will use vague or socially sentimental numbers. We need criteria of social efficiency that are as precise as possible. It is, for instance, of some moment whether the potential users of a water project will be able to sustain the cost of that project. It may well be necessary to subsidize directly some function or region, but the subsidy should be clearly labeled as such, not smuggled in, disguised as a hard and serious number.

There is already a horrendous example of this latter procedure. The "tax expenditure" budget of the federal government now allocates over $200 billion by exempting various categories of taxpayers in order to encourage them to behave in a certain way. This has meant, as numerous studies have demonstrated, that some "inefficient" investments are made "efficient" by virtue of the Internal Revenue Code, and vice versa. The left has argued persuasively that these indirect grants should be abolished and that Congress, when proposing a subsidy, should be required to appropriate money openly and directly. The advocates of democratic planning have to be as rigorous with themselves as they are with corporations. If, as in my hypothetical case, a subsidy was the least costly investment, it could still be paid—but explicitly designated as such and regularly reviewed.

I am not arguing here against bias in planning, since *some* bias is unavoidable, but rather for making such bias open and therefore subject to debate. One of the merits of the Rebuilding American Program put out by the International Association of Machinists (IAM) is that it makes perfectly clear its bias in favor of unionists, blacks, women, and the poor. Its program calls for a Federal Investment Reserve Fund and a pension fund development bank that would operate on a social calculus. The money for the Fund would come from an economic and social dividend to be paid by private corporations from after-tax profits. This, in itself, immediately and sharply distinguishes the IAM proposals from other suggestions for a national investment fund —say Felix Rohatyn's, which would just put the taxpayer's money at the disposal of giant companies.

Still more to the point, the IAM argues that the chairperson of the planning institution ought to be a trade unionist, a profound challenge to the accepted practices which raises a crucial point. No one in the United States thinks it strange that public bodies with enormous power should be run by boards totally composed of bankers and businesspeople (the Federal Reserve System; New York's Municipal Assistance Corporation). It is indeed true, as old Calvin Coolidge said, that the business of America is business. Or, more precisely, it has been true. But if this country is being dragged into an explicit politicalization of more and more economic decisions—above all, investment decisions—we can no longer live by the old rules.

The IAM suggestion sharply dramatizes this point. In a transition of this magnitude, the elected representatives of the working people have a moral and political right to play a special role. So do consumers, minorities, women, and other constituencies. None of them, however, is as clearly organized and represented as working people. What is at issue in proposing that a unionist chair the planning body is a recognition that planning is an area of conflict; that corporate domination of planning is a way to compound rather than solve a crisis; and that what we are discussing is a radical new political departure, not simply the creation of some kind of planning "mechanism."

This leads me to a final point in my description of the planning process: its politicization. Alternate plans should be presented to the public. That there will be disagreement is, I think, not only inevitable but desirable. If, as the International Association of Machinists suggests, one component of the plan would be a program for exports (linked with a commitment to modernizing the Third World), different regions and industries would have different estimates of what should be done. That is what happens right now in our uncoordinated, incoherent, backdoor "planning." Various sectors of the economy lobby for *their* tax breaks, quite often supported by *their* unions, and that is one reason why government intervention is such a patchwork. But now these conflicts would be explicit, a subject for public debate, a part of the political life of the nation.

All the details I have imagined here are *illustrations* of ideas that might also be implemented in some other way. But are these fundamental ideas practical?

All imagined futures must seem to be utopian; only the present is really plausible. But consider the radical change which has already taken place and which is clearly only a prelude to even more sweeping transformations. Can one imagine a democratic planning process decreasing the destruction of the South Bronx and a good part of Detroit and St. Louis? Yet an undemocratic planning process has already done precisely that.

Does democratic planning mean the nationalization of the American economy? No. Wholesale nationalization is not today a politically serious proposal in the United States—or, for that matter, in European countries, which have had much more experience with, and are much more positive toward, public property. We now know that transferring title from a private to a governmental entity does not necessarily change much. Indeed, the transfer of title is only a prelude to the serious question: who exercises the public's ownership and on what basis? The Tennessee Valley Authority (TVA) must be counted one of the great successes of American social policy, an example of effective regional planning. At the same time, it must be acknowledged that the TVA was largely responsible for the strip-mining of Appalachia and in this regard acted no better, and perhaps even worse, than private utilities. And it has been—is— one of the chief proponents of a "breeder" reactor which is both environmentally and economically wrong.

But if one thus rejects simplistic notions about public property as a remedy for all ills—and realizes that a cadre of competent, motivated social-cost accountants capable of running a public enterprise is yet to be created—that does not mean that the public sector has no role to play. It most emphatically does. There are areas of social need where the start-up costs are so huge that private corporations refuse to invest in them without public financing, particularly when the "paper entrepreneurship" of speculative games is so much more lucrative.

The characteristic procedure nowadays—obviously delightful for corporate power—is that, even with public financing, the corporations retain the right to design the enterprise on the basis of "private" decisions. Here, again, politics comes to the fore. Technology is not simply technological; it always embodies values and assumptions about the worth of the people who produce and use it. One of the functions of democratic planning should be to have input, not simply about the "gross" aggregates of the GNP, but about the qualitative national product as well. Indeed, one tragedy of the present situation is that working people, faced with a choice between no job and work in a carcinogenic enterprise that might shorten their lives, will understandably choose the latter alternative. That is why, for instance, some unions have joined with corporations in opposing or weakening environmental standards. Elitists might simply excoriate labor for its "insensitivity"; a serious approach would make decent choices possible.

If, for instance, Exxon contracted to develop solar energy for the United States, it would most likely invent a centralized, large-scale technology, one designed to keep the sun under corporate control as far as that is possible. But it could be the goal of a public enterprise developing solar energy to do so in a way that would allow the technology to be small-scale, usuable in American homes and communities *and* in places like Tanzania and Bangladesh. To say this is obviously much more difficult than to do it, not least because one would need competent engineers who could translate a vision of human potential into an efficient, useful product.

Indeed, solar energy is precisely one of the areas in which the establishment of a TVA–type corporation might both generate jobs and provide important, humanely designed goods and services to a public willing and able to pay for them. High-speed rail service is another case in point. In 1979, the Joint Economic Committee of the Congress agreed that it was necessary to create entire new industries to replace the jobs of industries which were becoming obsolete or relatively unprofitable. The Joint Economic Committee found an economic potential for high-speed railroads like those that already exist in France, Britain, and some twenty regions of Japan. Putting such a system together would, of course, provide useful work for tens of thousands of Americans over an entire generation.

But, again, who would supervise this undertaking? The management of the American railroads—Penn-Central, for instance —is historically ingrown and unimaginative (characteristics it shares with steel management). It would be absurd to invite the executives who ruined the old rail system to take charge of building a new one. Here, too, there is a strong pragmatic argument for creating regional rail corporations on the TVA model and designing them to pay for their cost over the long term like any other major infrastructural investment.

Despite all the qualifications I have made with regard to the public sector, it has one enormous advantage. The investment is directly social. Federal monies appropriated to build a rail system will not be spent on buying oil companies. That the investment is social can be made all the more certain if the public enterprises are organized in a democratic way, with worker and consumer representatives on the boards of directors. Creating a transparent and participatory management mechanism does not, of course, "guarantee" the right result: TVA made those decisions about buying coal from the strip mines of Appalachia in sessions which were, like all TVA board meetings, open to the public. But this structure of management remains an essential and promising first step.

An expansion of the public sector would be one way of implementing a democratic plan. The use of pension funds for social purposes is another. In 1982, pension funds were estimated to be worth $800 billion. That means, at present, that about 25 percent of all stock and 40 percent of corporate bonds are held by these funds.

There are four major types of pension funds: (1) federal government; (2) state and local government; (3) corporate employer-controlled funds; and (4) jointly administered (trade union and management) funds, which may include multi-employer plans. The federal plans have about $120 billion in assets, exclusively held in treasury securities and bonds, or about 12 percent of the national debt. The state and local funds, which often include employee representatives, control about $200 billion in corporate bonds and stocks, treasury issues, and in some cases, mortgages. The corporate-controlled funds are the largest single component of the whole, with $400 billion in assets. Only half of these funds are subject to collective bargaining; the rest are completely under the control of non-union (and often, anti-union) interests. Finally, the jointly controlled funds, found mainly in competitive industries with many individual firms (textiles, garment, construction), total between $50 billion and $90 billion.

These huge sums of money earned extremely low yields between 1965 and 1979, with a total annual return of 4.1 percent in a period when inflation averaged 6.2 percent. Moreover, there were handsome investments of nominally worker-owned funds in anti-union enterprises like Texas Instruments, IBM, and J.P. Stevens. Wouldn't it, then, be relatively simple to put this money under actual worker or union control and to utilize it in job-generating, socially useful investments?

Unfortunately, it would not. What do workers want from their pension funds? Secure pensions paying the highest possible benefits. If, then, one really became participatory in determining how these funds are to be used and consulted the nominal owners, would they freely choose a socially responsible, but risky, investment path? Or even a socially responsibe, but low-yielding, path? The questions almost answer themselves. Compound this problem with a related difficulty: if workers' retirement funds were being used in a socially responsible way, would that free bankers to put their dollars into socially irresponsible and quite profitable investments? Does the pension fund strategy lead to cream for the rich and curdled milk for the people?

That question is not fanciful. In the mid-seventies, the New York City banks played a major role in creating the municipal fiscal crisis—benefiting from inside information and dumping the city paper that they had helped create when they saw bad times coming. They then refused to put a nickel of their reserves into saving the city. The municipal unions, however, did come to the rescue and switched monies from out of other securities and into the city coffers. As it turned out—and as could have been predicted—it was a shrewd investment for the unions. But isn't this a paradigm of how workers' retirement benefits could be bilked in the name of social utility? Quite possibly.

Fortunately, there are ways to deal with this problem. It has been proposed that Washington create a new, fully guaranteed security that a national development bank devoted to reindustrializing the nation could then sell to union pension funds. Since the security would be fully guaranteed, the funds would be protected under the "prudent man" rule (that the decisions of fund trustees be those of a "prudent man"). If this were done, some UAW analysts have pointed out, the unions would also have a certain leverage over development bank policy, since they could buy or not buy its securities according to how they evaluated the investments it was making.

Another interesting suggestion in this area comes from a Pension Investment Unit set up by former Governor Jerry Brown in California. The Unit has done some important and practical work in devising intelligent ways for getting pension funds into socially useful projects. The Unit also offers an example of how a public institution can put expertise and computers at the service of unions and municipalities to help them make better decisions. It conceived of itself as a kind of public-interest "broker," in both the narrow (stock market) and broader meanings of that term.

There are a whole series of institutions, the Unit notes, designed over the past forty years to channel capital into housing, a sector that the government, making a planner's choice, had designated as a priority for investment. There were the federal agencies like the Federal Housing Authority (FHA) and Veterans' Administration (VA), the Government National Mortgage Association (GNMA, or "Ginny Mae"), the Federal National Mortgage Association (FNMA, or "Fanny Mae") and so on. The California Unit suggests a new entity: "Teddie Mac," the Technology Development and Mortgage Assurance Corporation. "The aim of Teddie Mac would be to increase the flow of pension capital and other institutional capital into small- and medium-scale firms by creating a security that meets investor requirements for safety, liquidity and return."

All of these proposals, it must be said, could be legislated without any commitment to national economic planning. Yet it should be clear by now that the decisions of democratic pension funds would be much more effective, *from the beneficiary's point of view* as well as that of society as a whole, if there were effective macro-economic planning at the national level. At the same time, the "Teddie Mac" concept demonstrates that an imaginative pension fund strategy need not focus exclusively on massive investments but could also channel resources to medium- and small-sized enterprises.

Let me add a word about employee-owned businesses. Until recently, the few examples of employee ownership in the United States were more nominal than real. In recent years a number of trends have changed this situation somewhat. Corporations bent on eliminating "inefficient" plants—inefficient, that is, by a corporate calculus—offered workers the opportunity to "buy out" the ownership. That often meant taking huge wage cuts in order to acquire a facility already run into the ground by private management. Or it meant an "ownership" in which the costs were real (that is, there was a decline in the workers' standard of living) but the benefits were questionable. In some cases, however, trade unionists carried through a "buy out" which was economically viable and involved a significant measure of rank-and-file control. One consequence of the shift in ownership was a marked increase in productivity. In this area, the existence of a pool of pension fund resources, democratically controlled by the beneficiaries and their institutions, could provide, with proper guarantees, significant financial support for transforming ownership patterns from the bottom up, rather than from the top down.

Yet the top-down approach is still important, particularly when one looks at another area of planning policy: the money system. Monetary policy provides a mechanism for allocating—or misallocating—capital for investment.

Beginning in October 1979, the Federal Reserve in effect declared itself agnostic on the subject of interest rates. It would —and it is worth remembering that this shift was carried through by a Carter appointee—focus exclusively on monetary aggregates and let interest rates rise or fall as they might. This involved a problem since, as the Council of Economic Advisors in its 1983 report freely admits, banks were playing so many games—NOW accounts, super NOW accounts, and so forth— that no one was sure what the money supply was. As a result, there was a redefinition of M1 (traditionally, cash and demand deposits) as M1-B in 1981, and then new redefinitions of M1 and M2 in 1982 and early 1983 in an attempt to deal conceptually with the banks' inventiveness in coming up with new forms of money.

All of this was, of course, compounded by an international money market crisis, as Poland and other East European countries and then oil-rich Mexico and Venezuela effectively went into bankruptcy. At the same time that Reagan's Council of Economic Advisors was arguing for further cuts in social programs, it was advocating government intervention to provide a "safety net for the international financial system." Meanwhile, joblessness rose dramatically in those sectors where interest rates are a critical factor in consumer demand—autos and housing; exports declined as the dollar rose; and foreigners poured money into the United States to take advantage of risk-free, guaranteed profits.

All this reinforces the point made at the outset: *the question*

*is not whether there is to be government intervention, but what
kind, under whose control, and for whose benefit.* The American
money system is a perfect case in point. In one way or another,
Washington—the Federal Reserve above all—has been allocating resources through the manipulation of interest rates. Housing
was the recipient of all kinds of subsidies that had the effect of
misallocating resources to the upper middle class and the rich.
Certainly we have been living with bad planners' choices in the
area of monetary policy. What we need are good planners'
choices.

There are a number of ways to achieve that goal. First, the
Federal Reserve should be reformed. The Chairperson of the Fed
should have a term that coincides with the President's; the mem-
bership of the Board should be opened up to nonbankers; interest
rates should be targeted; and there should be a legislative re-
quirement that Fed policies reinforce the priorities of elected
officials in the executive and legislative branches. All of these
procedural transformations are, however, simply a means to an
end: *the allocation of credit in accord with social priorities.*

In recent years there has been a deafening chorus from the
right—and from "neoliberal" Democrats—chanting that all of
our economic problems are due to an inadequate rate of savings
and investment. At the same time that corporate investors were
said to be "crowded out" of the money markets, there was an
endless supply of capital for corporate take-overs and other speculative uses. The real issue, however, was not the *supply* of capital but its *misallocation.* And a chief promoter of speculative
waste was the Federal Reserve itself.

As part of the planning process advocated here, there should
be differential interest rates whose level is determined by the
use to which the borrowed money is put. Note well: differential
interest rates already exist; they have functioned in housing for
almost half a century. The point is now to apply the social calculus urged earlier to the money system itself, to establish, in simple
terms, a prohibitive interest rate on loans for corporate take-
overs; a supportive interest rate for the housing of working
people and the middle class (financed in part by "capping" the

deductibility of mortgage interest at $10,000); and a supportive interest rate for people buying low- and medium-priced cars.

Finally, the area of subsidies to corporations provides another illustration of how a democratic planning policy can be multi-faceted in its execution. Robert Reich, one of our most interesting policy analysts, has much that is excellent to say on this topic—and some things that are dangerous. Reich sees planning as the centralized drafting of detailed blueprints for the economy—and rejects it. But it should be quite clear by now that what is suggested here is much more complex, decentralized, and participatory than this notion of centralized planning. Still, at the same time that Reich rejects "planning" as defined (I would say, mis-defined) in that narrow fashion, he is quite shrewd in his account of the basic transformations now taking place. The advanced economies, he writes, are moving from a technology that produced long runs of standardized products to a technology that will focus on small batches of more specialized products. The American future, he says, lies in high-value "niches" in heavy industry (steel, chemicals), as well as in new forms of technology (biotechnology, robotics, and so forth).

With this analysis, Reich comes to important conclusions about the nature of work and the proper response to the current crisis. With this new and very specialized technology, the hier-archical organization of work becomes a fetter upon production. Teamwork and cooperation are no longer values for moralists to preach but imperatives of efficiency. This means that society must be prepared to make a much larger investment in human capital which under these new circumstances, becomes a key to dealing with our plight.

So far, so good. Even when Reich goes on to argue for sub-sidies to corporations that agree to train workers to be able to cope with this unprecedented technology, I can see his point. But his refusal to think in terms of a decentralized and participatory planning imposes sharp limits upon Reich's analysis and pro-gram. Government, he says, will help business adjust to the new technology, but not through a patchwork of grants and tax de-ductions. Rather, it will make a contract with the corporations:

they will agree to restructure and to retrain their existing work-force, either at changed jobs in the present industry or in jobs opened up in new industries. Indeed, the corporations will replace the welfare state as the locus for the provision of social services that will be, in part, under workers' control. All employees and their dependents, Reich asserts, will become employee-members of some business enterprise.

This is, I fear, a kind of industrial feudalism, and I have many problems with it. Enterprises vary in productivity and success. Does that mean that the social services provided by the newest, highest-output enterprises will be superior to those in the more backward plants? Small, the French socialist Jean-Pierre Cot remarked recently, is not always beautiful; it is sometimes greedy and competitive. Will the corporate centers of society, even with the most extensive workers' control, become agencies of a kind of collective capitalism? And where is the notion of certain basic and universal rights—to health care, retirement benefits, and the like? If the answer to these questions is that the society will have to adjust for the differentials, then one is back at . . . planning. If not, one has conjured up a technologically developed feudalism, the Japanese present writ large as the American future.

One of the tools of planning should indeed be "contracts" with corporations. To begin with, although my ultimate goal is the abolition of the large private corporation—I think that all major economic decisions should be made democratically and that there should be no private-propertied right to make decisions which govern the lives of people who have no role in making them—the fact is that the corporation is going to be around for the foreseeable future. But corporations can be brought into the plan; they need not *necessarily* dominate it. The "normal" tendency of a society in which corporations retain a major influence over basic investment decisions is for them to dominate the society, including its democratic political institutions. That is why every proposal in this essay suggests democratic intrusions upon that corporate economic power. One of those ways is to make all federal subsidies not simply transparent and labeled as such but conditional upon achieving specified social goals. If a corporation does create new jobs in an area of high unemployment, then double the investment tax credit; if it takes jobs out of such an area, eliminate the investment tax credit. The hidden subsidy process has until now served to reward irresponsible corporate behavior; an open, democratic subsidy process will provide resources for socially responsible behavior.

Many of the proposals I have made here could be adopted piecemeal whether or not America moves to national economic planning. But such an approach to reform would replicate some of the worst aspects of the existing welfare state in America.

Our welfare state was the last to be established in the advanced capitalist world. Moreover, it is the cheapest in the West, spending a smaller percentage of Gross National Product on social goals than any European nation. Finally, the American welfare state is distinctively individualist. It does not provide universal rights, like national health care; it certainly does not act in a redistributive fashion. It provides a "safety net"—tattered, in the era of Ronald Reagan—for individuals who fall out of a system that, it is piously and mistakenly believed, guarantees the needs of almost all citizens.

Yet this rag-tag welfare state can be very costly. Ronald Reagan, who in one year will preside over a deficit higher than the sum of the deficits in Jimmy Carter's four years, is an eloquent witness. His own Council of Economic Advisors said in 1983 that a 1 percent increment in unemployment costs the society (in lost tax revenue and increased entitlements) $25 billion. That figure is, I think, quite low; the actual cost of 1 percent of unemployment is at least $30 billion—but let's not quibble. Even taking the Reaganite estimates, the costs of the increase in joblessness have reached an annual rate of over $100 billion. Put another way, if unemployment in January of 1983 were at the 1980 rate, Reagan's deficit would be half of what it is; if the economy were at the Kennedy-Johnson definition of full employment (4 percent unemployment), the federal budget would be in surplus!

Reagan blames the entitlements for our situation, since they were introduced by his predecessors. The real guilt lies, of course, with the Reaganite policies that triggered the drain on the entitlements: *our problem is not unemployment compensation but unemployment*. Still, what do we get for our huge outlays? Very little. In Europe and Japan, by contrast, as Robert Reich points out, social services are seen not as reluctant concessions to unfortunate individuals, but as a means of shaping a new labor force in a changing economy.

Let me be specific. When I was in Pennsylvania in the winter of 1983 talking to unemployed steel workers, I discovered some of the reasons why they were unable to take advantage of employment openings in other parts of the country. The people I talked to had, in almost every case, a mortgaged house. If they were to pull up stakes and leave in search of jobs, they would have to put that house on the market in an area with 20 percent, and even 25 percent, unemployment. Where would the buyers come from? Yet if there were a national housing policy and a national full employment policy, that problem could be eliminated. Those workers lucky enough to retain health care coverage under the union contract were similarly tied to the area and its industry. But if there were national health care, they would be better able to risk the changes.

We should stop thinking about welfare in individualistic terms and start to think of it as an enormous pool of funds that could be used to retrain, to relocate, to generate work. The solution to the short-run problem of joblessness could, and should, be an element in a long-run program to transform America's economic structure. But that requires national planning.

A related and even more radical point is found in Wassily Leontief's *Scientific American* article. It has to do with income distribution, the length of the working year, and technological change. Twenty years ago, Leontief writes, the creation of an additional job required $50,000; now it costs $100,000; and in twenty years, even discounting for inflation, it could reach $500,000. One cannot, he continues, deal with that problem by massively slowing down the rate of technological change, for that would deprive us of the output we need. How, then, to confront the fact that the latest copper smelter to go into service in the

United States cost $450 million and employs fewer than 50 workers per shift?

If, Leontief notes, this country had decreased the working week and increased the real wages of workers over the past generation, it could have absorbed even this kind of technological change without intolerable unemployment rates. The "Automation Commission" of the 1960s held that it was necessary only to fine-tune the monetary and fiscal aggregates in order to adapt to any rate of technological change. But Leontief argues—and history sustains him—that what was needed was social and institutional change, not technocratic fine-tuning. Now, he goes on, it is too late. If we suddenly made up for all that we should have done and did not do—cut hours drastically and maintain or raise wages at the same time—that "would require such a large increase in the share of total national income going to wages that it would bring decline in productive investment. . . ."

But we could, Leontief continues, try to achieve the same result through an incomes policy that would transfer some share of the (upper) incomes to blue-collar and white-collar workers—through social programs, among other mechanisms—and thereby compensate them for individual wages lost through reduced hours of work. Leontief introduces an illuminating analogy. Half a century ago, he writes, the farm family worked from dawn until dusk with a team of horses and perhaps a tractor. Their income consisted of what was essentially a wage for a seventy-five- or eighty-hour week, supplemented by a small profit on their investment. Today, that same farm family has a much larger investment in machinery, and consequently their work time is much shorter. But their total wage income, "if one computes it as the going hourly rate for a much smaller number of manual labor hours, is probably not much higher than it was fifty years ago and may even be lower. Their standard of living, however, is certainly much higher: the shrinkage of their wage income is more than fully offset by the income earned on their massive capital investment in the rapidly changing technology of agriculture."

In the farm sector, this result was produced without planning. In the industrial—and postindustrial—sectors, it will not happen automatically, but only through an incomes policy and a new attitude toward the relative value of leisure time and money. The old debate over income distribution takes on a new dimension. It is not simply a matter of abstract right, of equity, to reduce the outrageous income and wealth inequalities of American society. That short-run goal is now an essential element in a long-range strategy for adapting America to a technology that is not compatible with either the forty-hour week or wages reached by purely private bargains. These short-range programs are already on the trade union agenda and point the way to long-range planning in perspective.

What is being urged here, both in an immediate and an intermediate context, is a large step beyond the New Deal. The New Deal assumed that the corporate infrastructure was sound, that the board room was the best place for the efficient allocation of economic resources. The New Deal welfare state accordingly contented itself with the minimal manipulation of fiscal and monetary aggregates to create an environment in which corporations could go on making their benign allocations. That reform did more for the American people than any innovation in the nation's history; but the system that it created is incapable of dealing with the sweeping transformation of the world division of labor, the technological revolution, and the internationalization of capital now under way. What is needed now is, among other things, a system of national economic planning that goes as far beyond the New Deal as the New Deal went beyond Herbert Hoover.

To recapitulate the specifics: democratic and participatory planning would:

- be based on a national needs inventory made at the community as well as at the national level;
- involve macro-economic, input-output analysis of how the technological revolution and the changing international division of labor will affect the economy and society;
- provide funds for counter-planning: public monies for critics

and opponents of the plan, so that they can have access to the technical competence to formulate their alternatives to it;

• develop, in the most rigorous possible way, social concepts of investment efficiency;

• be at least as biased in favor of working people, minorities, women, and other democratic constituencies as the present (shamefaced) planning system is biased in favor of corporations;

• within a reasonable time, provide for the reindustrialization of the "rust bowl" in the industrial Northeast and Midwest;

• be committed to help the modernization of the Third World, with the aim of eliminating the structural inferiority of the South in the world economy.

This decentralized, democratic planning process would provide the framework for the elaboration of some plan(s). Among the measures that could implement the priorities arrived at in this way might well be included:

• an expansion of direct public-sector investment in areas like solar energy and high-speed regional rail systems;

• the use of pension funds, with federal guarantees, as a source of socially responsible investment capital, and the creation of public "brokers" with the expertise to advise on the best way of investing these monies;

• the facilitation of genuine employee ownership and control of enterprises;

• the reform of the Federal Reserve system and the allocation of credit on the basis of social efficiency;

• the practice of making all subsidies to private corporations (tax expenditures or direct outlays) contingent upon the actual implementation of the priorities of the plan(s);

• the utilization of welfare payments as part of an overall investment in human capital, rather than as a system providing minimal (and subminimal) protection for individuals;

• the reduction of the working day, paid for, in part, by transfer payments within the framework of an incomes policy.

Planning is coming. Indeed, it is already here; and those who deny that fact, whether out of innocence or guile, are the true crackpots of the age. The real issue before us is not whether there will be planning but who will plan, how, and for what purposes. These few suggestions for immediate, practical reforms could move our nation, even if very slowly, toward a decentralized and democratic determination of the basic economic decisions that shape our lives.

Biographical Note on the Contributors

IRVING HOWE is the author of *World of Our Fathers, A Margin of Hope*, and, most recently, editor of *1984 Revisited: Totalitarianism in Our Century*. Co-editor of *Dissent* magazine, he is also a professor of English at the Graduate Center, City University of New York.

BOB KUTTNER is a social and economic analyst. Former editor of *Working Papers*, he is now contributing editor to *The New Republic*.

BARBARA EHRENREICH is a feminist leader, co-author of *For Her Own Good*, and author of *The Hearts of Men*.

FRANCES FOX PIVEN is a social analyst and, with Richard Cloward, co-author of *Regulating the Poor* and *The New Class War*. She is a professor of political science at the Graduate Center, City University of New York.

GORDON ADAMS is the director of the Center on Budget and Policy Priorities, Washington, D.C., and author of *The Politics of Defense Contracting*.

ROBERT LEKACHMAN is an economist and professor of economics at City University of New York. He is the author of *Greed Is Not Enough*.

MICHAEL HARRINGTON is a socialist leader and political commentator. He is a professor of sociology at Queens College and the author of *The Other America, The Accidental Century*, and *Socialism*.